Early Praise for *Create Mobile Games with Corona*

It's straightforward, it's thorough, and it walks new users through all of the basics. I especially like how the book explains full game templates for popular genres in an easy-to-understand way.

➤ **Brent Sorrentino, developer liaison at Corona Labs**

I've wanted to make an iPhone game since the launch of the App Store, and now I feel like I'm closer to my goal. The Corona SDK is a powerful tool, but good tutorials are hard to find; I feel much more prepared having read Silvia's book!

➤ **Stephen Orr, lead developer at Made Media**

Looking for a way into programming mobile devices? What could be more fun than making a game (or three)? *Create Mobile Games with Corona* inspired me to get a little further with an idea I had for a mobile app, and Corona offers lots of speed and versatility for creating such things.

➤ **Stephen Wolff, Django developer**

Do you want to develop games for the Android platform? Look no further. This book teaches you to create ready-to-distribute games in Lua in no time. Highly recommended!

➤ **Brian Schau, developer, Rovsing Applications**

Create Mobile Games with Corona

Build with Lua on iOS and Android

Silvia Domenech

The Pragmatic Bookshelf

Dallas, Texas • Raleigh, North Carolina

Many of the designations used by manufacturers and sellers to distinguish their products are claimed as trademarks. Where those designations appear in this book, and The Pragmatic Programmers, LLC was aware of a trademark claim, the designations have been printed in initial capital letters or in all capitals. The Pragmatic Starter Kit, The Pragmatic Programmer, Pragmatic Programming, Pragmatic Bookshelf, PragProg and the linking *g* device are trademarks of The Pragmatic Programmers, LLC.

Every precaution was taken in the preparation of this book. However, the publisher assumes no responsibility for errors or omissions, or for damages that may result from the use of information (including program listings) contained herein.

Our Pragmatic courses, workshops, and other products can help you and your team create better software and have more fun. For more information, as well as the latest Pragmatic titles, please visit us at *http://pragprog.com.*

The team that produced this book includes:

Fahmida Y. Rashid and Aron Hsiao (editors)
Potomac Indexing, LLC (indexer)
Candace Cunningham (copyeditor)
David J Kelly (typesetter)
Janet Furlow (producer)
Juliet Benda (rights)
Ellie Callahan (support)

Printed in the United States of America.
ISBN-13: 978-1-937785-57-4
Printed on acid-free paper.
Book version: P1.0—November 2013

Contents

Part III — Vertical-Scrolling Shooter

Part IV — Tower Defense

Part V — Physics and Distribution

Acknowledgments

I would like to begin by thanking the artists who have made this book's projects possible. Without them, the demos would be limited to stick figures created by an artistically challenged programmer. I am indebted to Daniel Cook from Lost Garden for his 2D tile set;[1] Cliff Harris from Positech Games for his explosion generator;[2] Lamoot and Luke.RUSTLTD from OpenGameArt, who shared their user-interface assets and crates, respectively;[3,4] and my father, Gabriel Domenech, who painted the spaceships, planets, and backgrounds used throughout the book. Thanks to Kibblesbob and Mike Koening at SoundBible for their missile and bomb sounds and to Kevin MacLeod at Incompetech for his Space Fighter Loop and Pinball Spring music loops.[5,6]

I must also thank the amazing community of developers who code using Corona, as well as all the beta readers who caught numerous bugs and made suggestions on the forums. This book also received lots of input from a great group of technical reviewers: in no particular order, they are Brent Sorrentino, Charley Stran, Javier Collado, Stephen Wolff, Al Scherer, Stephen Orr, and Brian Schau. Of course, this book is what it is thanks to my editors, Fahmida Y. Rashid and Aron Hsiao, both exceptional in different ways. Finally, thanks to the Pragmatic Programmers for their wonderful writing workflow and everything they do for the programming community...oh, and for letting me write this book!

---

1.   http://www.lostgarden.com
2.   http://www.positech.co.uk
3.   http://opengameart.org/users/lamoot
4.   http://opengameart.org/users/lukerustltd
5.   http://www.soundbible.com
6.   http://incompetech.com/

Preface

Greetings and welcome to the world of mobile-game development! If you're reading this, then you're probably already aware of the Corona SDK and its usefulness for mobile app development and mobile games in particular.[1] In this book, you'll learn Corona by developing a series of mobile games, mastering most of Corona's capabilities in the process. We'll start with a relatively simple game and some basic mechanics and then quickly move on to more complex games and techniques. By the time we're done, you'll be able to code interactive games with moving units and projectiles and even include advertisements and high scores.

Corona? Why Corona?

The Corona SDK is a great tool for making 2D mobile games. It's cross-platform, it's easy to learn, and it makes it really fast to code games. You can also forget about buying expensive programs and tools before you get started, because Corona lets you code and distribute your games for free. You need to buy it only if you want to add advanced features such as in-game ads or in-game purchases.

Cross-Platform Development

Many game-development environments make it difficult for us to create games for multiple platforms. Even if we can port to multiple platforms, some of those games may not be optimized. When making mobile games, it's especially important to use as few resources as possible; we don't want users to see their battery life plummet the second they open our games. Corona lets us make games specifically targeted at mobile devices, both iOS and Android, so we won't be making lazy ports of PC games.

---

1. Corona and Corona SDK are registered trademarks of Corona Labs Inc.

Free Starter Edition

Corona's free starter edition is called Corona SDK Starter. Unlike many game engines' starter editions, it comes with almost all the features currently available in the Pro version. You can install the program, learn how to use it, and distribute your games with the free version. You don't have to buy Corona until your games are really good and you want to add advertisements or offer in-app purchases.

Quick Prototyping and Coding

You won't believe this until you get coding, but Corona makes coding much faster than if you decided to code directly in Objective-C or Java. You'll use Lua, and you can load and display an image with a single line of code. You can add physics to that image with another line. You can write great games using very little code.

Built-in Physics Engine

Corona comes with a Physics application programming interface (API) built on top of Box2D, which means you won't have to code your own physics behaviors and collision-detection functions. Adding physics to your games will be easy and quick. Debugging will be easy, too.

Great Developer Community

A wonderful community uses Corona. You can visit the official discussion boards to interact with other Corona programmers.[2] There are lots of tutorials and ready-made code samples for you to use while writing your games.

Who Should Read This Book?

This book is for aspiring game developers and mobile developers, especially those who want to develop polished, professional games for multiple platforms quickly and easily. Even if you're not a programming guru, you'll find it easy to code games using Corona with this book as your guide. You'll make the most out of this book if you know at least one programming language. If you're familiar with functions, variables, loops, and classes, then you're good to go.

What's This Book About?

In this book, you'll learn about Corona from scratch, so you only need to bring your enthusiasm, and we'll go through each of the steps together. Regardless of your previous programming experience, we'll work through this

---

2.   Access the Corona SDK forums at http://forums.coronalabs.com/.

book and make several games. In fact, if you're like me and would prefer to jump directly into action, you can install Corona and start building your first app in Chapter 2, *The Game Loop*, on page 17.

Figure 1—The book's projects

Over the course of this book, we'll build the games shown in the screenshots, but let's take a look at what you'll learn.

- In Chapters 2 through 4, in Part II, *Planet Defender*, on page 15, we'll develop a planet-defender game. Players will be in charge of destroying hordes of invading enemy ships. To achieve this, you'll learn how to write a game loop, add sprites, and accept basic player input.

- In Chapters 5 through 7, in Part III, *Vertical-Scrolling Shooter*, on page 69, we'll build a fast-paced vertical scroller. You'll learn how to add animation to game objects, sort objects into groups, and create perspective effects. We'll also talk more about sprites and object movement and enhance our interactivity techniques.

- After creating two space games in Parts II and III, we'll switch gears in Chapters 8 through 10, in Part IV, *Tower Defense*, on page 121, and build a fun tower-defense game instead. You'll learn to create waves of enemies, move them around the screen, and enable players to build towers to kill them. To make this work, we'll implement movement, pathfinding, shooting, and even progressive difficulty settings.

- In Chapters 11 and 12, in Part V, *Physics and Distribution*, on page 181, you'll learn advanced game-programming techniques in Corona. We'll make a basic physics-based game, and we'll add advertisements, high scores, achievements, and in-app purchases. We'll conclude the book with instructions for publishing our apps and releasing them into the world so all our cool new programs aren't doomed to oblivion on our hard drives. You'll need a Pro version of Corona to complete some activities in Chapter 12, but the Starter edition should be fine for everything else.

How to Read This Book

Nobody expects you to read a programming book the way you'd read a novel; you are not expected to read it from cover to cover. Instead, feel free to skip to those sections that interest you and go back if you have trouble with some of the concepts from previous chapters. You can also jump to the projects that interest you and read the explanations for the features you'd like to learn. If you're of the classic type and want to read the chapters consecutively, then you're welcome to do so.

Online Resources

As you work on the book's projects, you'll need to download the book's code files, found at http://pragprog.com/book/sdcorona/create-mobile-games-with-corona. There, you'll have access to the complete code projects built for this book.

You can also visit the section of the Pragmatic Forums dedicated to this book, found at http://forums.pragprog.com/forums/247.

Ready, Get Set, Go!

Now that you've reached this point, you're ready to get to the real action. You can start by reading Chapter 1, *Hello, Corona!*, on page 3, where we'll install Corona and create our first "Hello, Corona!" program, or you can skip directly to Chapter 2, *The Game Loop*, on page 17, and start coding our Planet Defender game.

Either way, fasten your seatbelts and get ready for the journey ahead. You're about to start learning Corona!

Part I

Getting Started

Before we get started with complex Corona projects, we have to install and configure the Corona SDK and learn how to use it.

CHAPTER 1

Hello, Corona!

Greetings, and welcome to *Create Mobile Games with Corona*. In this chapter, you'll learn how to install Corona, build a really small app to ensure the game engine works properly, and learn a bit about game development along the way.

In this book, you'll start learning about Corona from scratch and build several mobile games. If you want to jump ahead, you can install Corona and start working on your first app in Chapter 2, *The Game Loop*, on page 17. Stick around if you want to learn about the various terms we'll be using as we familiarize ourselves with Corona.

1.1 A Word on Game Development

Making games is both a rational activity and a creative endeavor. What does this mean? It's means that no matter how smart or skilled we may be, we can't just write an equation for fun, implement it in code, and end up with great, immersive gameplay. Technical skills are certainly involved, but making games also requires developers to have fun and express their creative sides. To transform ourselves into serious game developers, in other words, we'll have to imagine entirely fictional worlds, their characters, and their properties and then combine all of them with our technical skills before sharing them with others.

There is no clear scientific approach to creating a game from scratch. On the bright side, this means there's a lot of room in the game-development market for original games. By designing and programming our own games, we can have the same fun that world-building novelists have, along with the thrills that come from writing and debugging a complex program.

90 Percent Development, 90 Percent Polish

Programming games may seem similar to traditional programming, but there are some important differences. Yes, we'll write code and compile and debug programs. As game developers, however, we also have to focus on entertainment. Even if we manage to create a well-coded, well-rendered, bug-free game, players won't play it if it's not fun. On the other hand, players often take to a really fun game even if it has ugly graphics and isn't perfectly implemented behind the scenes.

To be solid game developers, we'll need to work with an eye toward making fun, playable games, not just writing great code. The best way to make sure that this happens is to enjoy what we're doing; if we're not enjoying the games as we make them, players probably won't enjoy our games, either. That's not to say that things never get tough. When coding, we'll encounter persistent bugs and intractable issues; problem solving and the implementation of workarounds are part of the programming cycle, so it's important to remember that game development doesn't end just because an initial prototype is working.

The prototype is just the beginning. For polished games, we'll have to expand our prototypes and convert them into full games and then refine them until we're happy with the results. This is different from nongame programming, in which we might focus on core functionality and bugs. This balancing, polish, and testing stage in a game's life cycle surprises novice game developers with the unexpected workload. If we're not careful, it can postpone launches by many months, so it's important to balance the "second 90 percent" of game development with a healthy dose of practicality. Once we're happy with our games and find them to be fun, it's often a good idea to launch them even if they aren't yet perfect and have bugs. We'll always be able to patch or release successors in the future. Otherwise, the polishing stage can wind up taking longer than the development stage.

Becoming a Game Developer

Many mobile games don't have a long list of contributors and specialists behind them. Since the number of developers tends to be small for mobile games, it's important to know at least something about programming if you want to make mobile games, because you'll sometimes end up doing a bit of everything, including working on the code, design, and art. You'll be in great shape if you've already used other programming languages, but don't worry if you don't have a broad set of programming skills. *Lua*, the language we use with Corona, is easy to learn, and this book will get you up to speed quickly.

Working through this book will develop the core tool set any mobile-game programmer needs.

Beyond gaining basic programming skills, prototyping is the first step in game development. As we gain proficiency with game programming in this book, we'll prototype several games with mechanics that can be used for many future game projects. It's always tempting to polish graphics and gameplay at this point, but our key goal for the prototyping stage will be to create games that work and can be played. The prototype tells us whether a game will ever be fun and identifies key changes that need to be made in subsequent development stages.

Graphics come after the prototyping stage. After nailing a fun prototype, it's usually time for us to come up with great graphics. On large development teams, there's often an artist in the group, but there are alternatives to this model. There are lots of free and paid resources for game graphics; Appendix 1, *Corona Resources*, on page 215, lists some of these, and we'll use them in various places in our examples. In this book, we won't let a lack of artistic ability prevent us from becoming successful mobile-game developers.

The testing stage follows everything else. We all have friends and family or know dedicated gamers who can play and provide feedback about a game. Paid testers are sometimes an option, but they certainly aren't necessary. The key difference between developing traditional software and games is in this stage. We want to fix gameplay or user-experience issues but not get bogged down trying to uncover or address every possible minor bug or gameplay balance issue. These issues are typically addressed using updates and patches after releasing the game.

After designing, coding, and testing games, we'll release them, instantly becoming mobile-game developers! Games that have a fun underlying concept and work reasonably well will have a lot of gameplays (also called *app sessions*), and the number will increase quickly. After a brief period to rest and regain energy, we can begin the development process again with a new idea for a game.

1.2 Getting Started with Corona

The Corona SDK is different from other programming environments. Instead of a workspace and an embedded debugging system, we'll be using a basic text editor to write code, and a graphics editor to make images. Corona will just be in charge of compiling and executing our games. To get started, we'll need both the Corona application programming interface (API) and a decent text editor. Over the next few pages, we'll cover the download, installation, and basic usage of Corona, and then we'll discuss some of the common text editors available to you, in case you don't already have a preferred one installed.

Downloading, Installing, and Meeting Corona

Feel free to use the trial version of Corona as we work through this book. Doing so won't limit your ability to follow along with all the projects. The trial shows a reminder every time we open the program, and excludes access to Corona's daily updates and app-publishing features, but those aren't really needed to learn Corona. We'll be able to complete all of the examples and do all of the exercises using the trial version.

To download Corona, visit the Corona SDK website and click the Download link.[1] You'll have to create an account. There's no workaround for this, so an email address and password are needed. Use something memorable because these details will be needed to run the Corona program. After registering, you'll see the page to download the program.

Installing Corona is user-friendly. Open your downloaded file and follow the instructions (click Next most of the time). Once Corona is installed, you'll be prompted for the username and password you created a moment ago. You'll be told how many days you've been using the trial version each time you open the program.

Once Corona has been installed, we're ready to begin. If you're using Windows, open the Corona simulator. If you're on Mac OS, open the Corona folder in the Applications folder and then open the Corona simulator to open Corona and reach the landing screen. If you want to see the console, open the Corona terminal instead.

The landing screen Corona displays at launch is intuitive. We can create a new project, run a local project in the simulator, monitor a dashboard with our games' statistics (although this feature is only for subscribers), or experiment with the array of demos that ship with Corona. There is also a set of links pointing us to the Corona community and documentation.[2] These links are useful if you want to meet fellow Corona developers or learn about a specific function.

---

1. Corona Labs: http://www.coronalabs.com/products/corona-sdk/
2. http://www.coronalabs.com

Creating a New Project

Let's create a new project in Corona, just to familiarize ourselves with the development process and the choices available. As you can see in the following screenshot, we're asked to enter an application name and to select the folder where we want to create our application. Then Corona offers us a choice of templates. We can choose from several options.

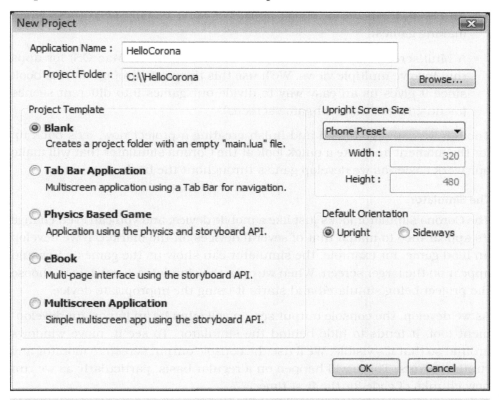

Figure 2—New project creation

- A Blank project template that provides an empty main.lua file. This is the template to use when writing an app from scratch. This can be a good choice for some single-screen games, but it is extra work for anything more complicated, meaning that we won't use it in this book.

- A Tab Bar Application template (called *App* on Mac OS) for creating apps with standard menu bars. Because we're focused on game development, we'll use our own custom menus most of the time, so we won't get much mileage out of this option either.

- A Physics Based Game template (called *Game* on Mac OS) for apps that leverage Corona's Physics API. This option gives us a basic app with physics support by default (though it's also possible to add Physics API support to projects that didn't start with this template). It also comes with storyboard support (like the multiscreen application) to simplify switching game scenes.

- An eBook template for ebook apps. We won't usually need these when making games.

- A Multiscreen Application template (called *Scene* on Mac OS) for apps that involve multiple views. We'll use this template throughout this book since it gives us an easy way to divide our games into different scenes (menus, levels, and end-game screens).

Though we could go ahead and finish creating a project now, let's back up for the moment and take a quick look at the Corona simulator that will make our work easier as we develop games throughout the book.

The Simulator

The Corona simulator looks just like a mobile device, and you can even change its appearance to match that of several devices on the market. If we develop an iPad game, for example, the simulator can show us the game as it would appear on the larger screen. When we open the simulator, it asks us to choose the project being simulated and starts it using the appropriate device.

As we develop, the console output screen will often be an important development tool. It tends to hide behind the simulator. To see it, move windows around so that it's visible. We'll use the console output screen to monitor any runtime errors. These will happen on a regular basis, particularly as we run new chunks of code for the first time.

The Dashboard

The dashboard is available only to subscribers, so we won't use it in this book. When it's time to release real mobile games into the wild and you decide to subscribe to Corona, then you will gain access to this area. Here you'll find stats for each of your released apps, including things like the total number of game sessions and the OS the player used to play each time. This will give you concrete data about your game's replay value and help you understand how your users are using your apps in the long run.

The Demos

Corona also comes bundled with an assortment of premade demonstration programs, each of which showcases one or two important features. As we work through the examples in this book, you'll gain confidence to be able to rip these apart and learn from additional examples. Some of the demos are great apps in their own rights and offer gameplay mechanics similar to those in some popular games.

Getting Official Corona Documentation

Like most programming environments, Corona offers extensive documentation. Corona's docs are wonderful learning tools because they usually offer detailed examples. Because the official docs are complete, you can use the official Corona SDK documentation to solve specific problems or fill knowledge gaps after we've finished working through this book.

Access the official Corona docs on the Corona website at www.coronalabs.com.

Choosing a Text Editor or Environment

If you don't already have a favorite text editor, you should consider picking one that highlights Lua code and shows line numbers. Any text editor will do as long as you can save Corona files with the proper extension (.lua). We'll spend most of our development time typing away in a text editor, so it's important that you choose one that feels comfortable to you. There are lots of options for programmers to choose from, but the following are three of the most popular free applications. In case you'd rather use a paid resource designed specifically for Corona, check out the ones listed in Appendix 1, *Corona Resources*, on page 215.

Eclipse

Platform: Mac OS or Windows

Eclipse is a great coding environment for many languages, and it also offers the option to make coding in Lua a lot easier because it highlights variables and color syntax as you code. Because of Lua's dynamic nature, spelling mistakes can lead to a lot of trouble during development, so a text editor that highlights variables can help reduce the number of frustrating mistakes.

Download Eclipse from http://www.eclipse.org/ and the Lua development tools from http://www.eclipse.org/koneki/ldt/.

Notepad++

Platform: Windows

If you're more fond of Notepad-style editors, choose Notepad++. It offers syntax highlighting and line numbers so that you can concentrate on coding rather than text details. It's also lightweight and launches quickly. It's not a development environment in the sense of Eclipse, but I use it to code 90 percent of my Lua programs.

Download Notepad++ from http://notepad-plus-plus.org/.

CodeMAX

Platform: Mac OS or Windows

CodeMAX is hosted at Lua Forge (meaning that it has a close relationship with the Lua community) and comes with syntax highlighting, code completion, and multilanguage support. It's similar to Notepad++, so making a choice between these two is really about aesthetics or selecting the tool layout that seems more intuitive to you.

Download CodeMAX from http://codemax.luaforge.net/.

1.3   Building Our First App

To get the ball rolling and test the Corona simulator at the same time, let's create a simple program that will draw ten rectangles on the screen. Not everything will make sense at this point, but you'll come to understand everything we do here over the next several chapters.

A Test Project

Open the Corona simulator, make a new blank project, and call it something like HelloCorona. This results in a file called main.lua that will hold our code. Navigate to the folder where you decided to create the project, and open the resulting file with your favorite text editor. From now on, we'll use the text editor to type our code, and each time we want to run the program we'll go back to the simulator and open it. You'll have to close the project in the Corona simulator if you want to make changes to some of the images and resources. Otherwise, they're considered "open" by the simulator, and you won't be able to update them.

The main.lua file that we'll be editing has some generated text already. You can either write immediately after it or replace it; both ways will work.

We want to draw some rectangles on the screen, so let's start writing in main.lua. We draw rectangles with Corona's display.newRect() function, so you would enter display.newRect(leftBorder, topBorder, width, height) to create some rectangle-drawing code. We could write something like this ten times to draw ten rectangles, but it's easier to use a loop. Enter for i = 1, 10 do before our rectangle-drawing code. If you've previously coded in other languages, this should be instantly familiar. If you haven't, don't worry, because you'll learn about loops in the next chapter. For now, let's just take a look at the code we've entered.

HelloCorona/main.lua

```
-- Draw 10 rectangles:
for i = 1, 10 do
    -- Draw a new rectangle at a random position,
    --     and with a random size and color
    local newRectangle = display.newRect( math.random(320),
        math.random(480), 10 + math.random(100), 10 + math.random(100) )
    newRectangle:setFillColor( math.random(255), math.random(255),
        math.random(255) )
end
```

This code will create ten random rectangles with different sizes and colors.

Testing Our App

Corona makes it really easy to compile and test apps. We don't need to download anything to an actual mobile device; to run our app, we just have to open it from the Corona simulator's menu. Apps in the simulator run just like on mobile devices. The only difference is that instead of tapping the screen with your finger, you'll use your computer's mouse.

Click the Simulate option on the simulator's starting screen, and navigate to the folder containing the app. To run an app, you just have to open its main code file, called main.lua. If there are several code files in a project, Corona will load them when they're required, so there's no need to open them explicitly in the simulator. Take a look at the following image to see what the simulator looks like.

If the app runs without errors, we know that Corona is installed correctly, and we're ready to get to work on other projects. If you face any issues compiling this project, double-check the spelling or take a look at the chapter's code files and try to run them. If you can't compile them either, then you may be facing post-installation issues in Corona. If that is the case, check your installation.

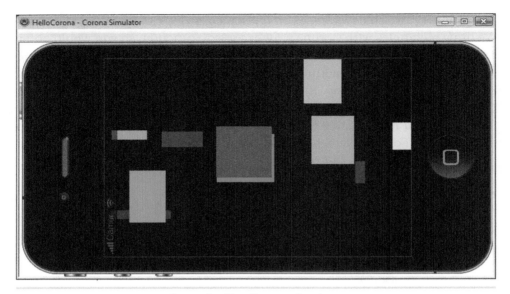

Figure 3—The Corona simulator

The Stage

If the code worked for you, you already have a running project. It's time to introduce a fundamental concept in Corona development: the stage. As we develop our games in the coming chapters, we'll draw a lot of things on the screen. In Corona, the device's screen is part of a graphical area called the *stage*. Think of the Corona stage the same way you'd think of a theater stage: anything that you add to the stage is intended for the audience (the player).

As is the case in theater, however, some things on the stage (say, at the end, in the wings) may be present and ready for use but not yet be visible to the audience. In Corona, we can do the same thing—draw things on the stage but outside the visible area of the screen. Corona automatically manages the stage and knows which things are on the visible part of the stage and which things are onstage but not yet visible. In this book (and in many other game-development contexts), we call the visible area of the device's screen the *screen bounds*. From now on we'll say that an object is "out of bounds" when it's on the stage but not yet visible to the player (not within the screen bounds).

We've just drawn our first ten rectangles on the stage (and within the screen bounds), as shown in the following image. In the coming chapters, we'll draw much, much more.

Figure 4—Our first app

Debugging

If the code in the test project didn't produce the expected result, it's time to check the console for error messages. Many other development environments stop everything whenever incorrect code is encountered. The Corona simulator usually keeps going, so errors and issues go undetected unless we monitor the console while running the project in the simulator. The console is where Corona prints all its error messages. Most of the errors are pretty straightforward English and may reference the specific function or command that is causing trouble. As a result, it's generally easy to tell by looking at an error what type of issue may be causing the problem.

Debugging just requires you to update your code and then run it again in the simulator. Sometimes it works after an easy change, but sometimes it doesn't. Luckily, as as a Corona developer, you'll soon learn to use the console to send yourself test messages while the code is running—everything from in-game data to "Everything is fine if we reached this far" messages—using the print function. You can also use the Debugger tool that comes with Corona and that can be used from some development environments like those listed Appendix 1, *Corona Resources*, on page 215.

1.4 What We Covered

Whew! We finished our first chapter. You learned a little about game development in general, installed Corona, ensured that it works, and even started some coding. At this point, you're ready to tackle games.

Not so sure? Feeling a bit overwhelmed? Don't worry. Coding games is easy once you get rolling, but everyone feels intimidated at the beginning. You'll get much more comfortable as we work through some mini-programs in the next few chapters. In *The Game Loop*, we'll start building something called a *game loop*, which we'll turn into a full-fledged game over the two chapters that follow.

And don't forget, the best part of making games is to have fun, so don't let yourself feel stressed. Enjoy the journey!

Part II

Planet Defender

In this project, we'll create a defense game focused on destroying spaceships that want to attack a planet. You'll learn how to start programming a game and about sprites and interactivity.

The Game Loop

Now that we've sprinted through the introduction and seen the lay of the land, it's time to get started with our first project. You don't need to know or understand everything in the first chapter by heart, but it's a good idea to have a working installation of Corona on your computer and to have played with a few of samples in the simulator a bit before beginning this chapter.

2.1 What You'll Learn

In this chapter, we'll start our first game project. We'll do the following:

- Design a small arcade game
- Create the basic layout for the game
- Learn the basics of Corona
- Experiment with the Lua programming language

Toward the end of the chapter, we'll focus on writing code that will update our game several times. By the end of the chapter, our app will look like the image shown earlier.

2.2 A Crash Course in Corona Programming

To program games, we need to be able to write programs. Now that we've installed Corona and made sure that it's working, we're ready to tackle the programming aspects. In this section, we'll create a new project to experiment with Lua, and then we'll move on to writing more game-specific code to gain experience with the development system.

The Console on Mac OS

If you're using Windows, then the Corona console appears automatically when you open the simulator. If you're working on Mac OS, you need to go to your Applications folder and open the Corona Terminal link. If you access the Corona simulator using the link on your Launchpad, then you won't automatically see the console.

Creating a Multiscreen Application

Let's start a new project in the Corona simulator so that we can test some of the basic options we have in the program. In Corona, we'll create a new project each time we want to create a new app.

Create a new multiscreen application (called *Scene* if you're on Mac OS), also known as a *storyboard* project in earlier versions of Corona. You can call it anything you like, but since we'll work on a game called Planet Defender, you may want to call it PlanetDefender.

The Corona Storyboard application programming interface (API) lets us divide an app into independent scenes, and each scene creates an empty image where we can add graphics and text. It's easier to use scenes for each part of an app, such as the main menu, the game, and the "game over" message. We can group related code to make it easier to write and debug, and we'll usually remove most images once we change scenes. By using a multiscreen application, we'll be able to swap from one of these sets of images and functions to another using Corona's scene-transitioning tools.

To create a multiscreen application, click the New Project button on the simulator. You'll get to the project-creation screen like you did in *Hello, Corona!*, and you'll only have to select Multiscreen Application as the project type. You'll get a file called main.lua and the main scene file, called scenetemplate.lua. If you want to change the scene's filename, you'll have to update the call to storyboard.gotoScene() in main.lua so that it calls the new name instead of the default scenetemplate.lua scene.

Each new scene file comes with four main functions, which Corona generates automatically for us as soon as we make a new project that uses the Storyboard API.

- createScene() will be called before showing the scene. Use this function to add content that has to appear right from the beginning of the scene.

- enterScene() will be called after showing the scene completely (in other words, after all the scene-transition effects). Use this to initialize a game or to add button effects.

- exitScene() will be called just before going out of the scene (in other words, before scene-transition effects). Use this to remove events, but don't remove visible objects yet.

- destroyScene() will be called once the scene is no longer visible. Use this function to remove images and other visible objects from the stage.

Writing on the Console

Our first tool in Corona will be the print() function, which prints any text or variable on the console. Remember that the console will always appear if you're using Windows, but you have to open the Corona terminal if you're using Mac OS.

To use the console, create a new project and type the following example in its main.lua, which calls print() and writes the word *message* on the console.

GameLoop/GameLoop_Console/main.lua
```
-- Print "message" on the console
print("message")
```

If you relaunch the program now (Ctrl+R), note the new text that has appeared on the console as we run our program. We've just called print() to write the word *message* on the console, but we can write anything else there.

To execute the program, you have to open the app from the Corona simulator. The console opens automatically when you run a project, but sometimes hides behind the simulator's screen. Drag it somewhere visible to see the output. In this case, you'll see the text *message*, which we passed as a parameter in the print() function.

As you can see in the following image, the print() function writes a message of our choosing on the console, which will make it easier for us to send ourselves messages as our program runs so that we can monitor what it's doing.

Figure 6—Printing on the console

As we discover bugs or problems with the programs we write, we'll add calls to this print() function in strategic places in the code and then relaunch the program and watch the console to see what it is doing.

You've probably noticed the lines preceded by -- in the sample code. This is how we indicate that the line is a comment and will not be processed by Corona. If you want to add notes to yourself within the code or just want to disable some function calls temporarily, you can add comments to do so.

Variables and Functions

Writing on the console is great, and *functions* like print() and others let us instruct the mobile device to do all kinds of things. But most of what goes on in a mobile game is more complicated than putting words on the screen. Functions give us a way to make our own complex lists of instructions, and *variables* will give us a way to hold the important information about our game world that our functions will use for decision making and important gameplay tasks.

Variables

Variables let us keep track of operations' results. We can store the number of lives a player has, keep count of the number of enemies on the screen, or even store the player's username. To define a variable, we type its name in Corona and assign a value to it. For example, we can write myFavoriteNumber = 12 to create a new variable called myFavoriteNumber.

Let's say we want to add a list of numbers and that we want to use that total number for something else. In this case, variables let us add them up once and then use the result as much as we want.

This is easier done than said, though, so let's write that function. We'll just add three numbers (1, 4, and 7) and store them as a variable called sumTotal. We'll then be able to print the total sum several times without having to recalculate the total every single time. Type the text from our example in a new project and see what happens.

GameLoop/GameLoop_Variables/main.lua

```lua
-- Add three numbers and store them in a variable
sumTotal = 1 + 4 + 7

-- Print the sum
print( sumTotal )
print( "in case you didn't see that, the total is " .. sumTotal )
```

When we run this code as shown, Corona first calculates the total using the normal addition operators and stores it in a variable called sumTotal. By using the print() command that we already talked about, the program then prints the total and prints it again in case we didn't notice it the first time around.

Figure 7—Variables in Corona

The second print() command in this example uses the string-concatenation operator in Lua, which lets you combine strings and variables. It's really useful for debugging.

Naming Variables

To name variables, you can use a lowercase letter for the start of the word and use a capital letter for every new word you use in the variable. For example, a variable holding my score would be called myScore.

You can use any other naming system you like, as long as it makes sense to you. We're game developers, so we're a bit like coding pirates (not software pirates, but those who pillage and plunder and live however they want to live). We can name variables in any way we like. Yarr! And if someone doesn't like it, we can throw them overboard to the sharks. Har, har! (Or we can agree to use a common naming convention if we really have to work with them...and there are no sharks nearby.)

Functions

In Lua, like in most programming languages, we can also create our own functions; we aren't limited to built-in functions like print(). By making our own functions and giving them names, we can create complex sets of directions or instructions that we can repeat over and over again anywhere in our code each time we call them by name. This saves us the hassle of rewriting a complex list of tasks each time we need to repeat it. We can execute a function whenever an enemy shoots or whenever the player loses a life. That way, we can avoid repeating code, and we can write neater programs.

In a simpler example, we might want to perform a complex mathematical operation for several numbers. We can write the operation each time, but it's much easier if we write it just once as a function and call it each time we want to apply the mathematical formula.

In Lua, we begin a list of instructions that we'd like to turn into a function using the function keyword. At the end of the list of instructions, we add the end keyword. We can even send messages to our functions that they can use in carrying out their instructions (like the text *message* that we sent to print(), which Corona then output on the screen). These are called *parameters* and act like variables that the instructions in our functions can use. We indicate that our function expects extra information (parameters) by enclosing names for them in brackets in the function definition.

By creating our own functions and letting them receive messages using parameters, we can easily perform basic lists of steps over and over again in our code, adapting them to individual cases. In Corona, we always have to write function definitions before calling the functions, because the code won't find them otherwise.

Let's build an example to illustrate the process. In this example we write a function that receives two numbers as its parameters and prints them to the console. We call the function printTwoNumbers(), and its parameters are number1 and number2. Again, we use the string-concatenation operator to combine the variables with readable text, to know what Corona has just printed on the console.

GameLoop/GameLoop_Functions/main.lua
```lua
-- Prints two numbers on the console
function printTwoNumbers( number1, number2 )
    print( "The two numbers are: "..number1.." and "..number2 )
end

-- Call the function
printTwoNumbers( 1, 2 )
printTwoNumbers( 4, 3 )
```

See how easy that was? Any time we want to print two numbers on the console, we call printTwoNumbers() and pass it the two numbers that we'd like to print, like the following figure shows. We can pass just about any pair of numbers as parameters and call the function from just about any part of our program with similarly useful results.

Figure 8—Functions in Corona

Local and Global Variables

So far, we've used variables to keep track of values. Corona also lets us define local and global variables for our games. In broad terms, local variables are accessible from wherever we define them (such as a function or code file) but not from an unrelated part of the program. Global variables are accessible from the entire program.

We might just need a variable during a short code fragment (such as within a function), so a local variable can be useful for that because it stops being useful outside the code and we can let Corona "forget" it. If we're keeping track of something gamewide or an app-configuration value, then it makes sense to use a global variable, because we'll likely need it later.

We can define a global variable by writing variableName = value, and *local* variables need the prefix local. In technical terms, the local keyword basically means that the variable won't be accessible from outside the area where we define it. If we place it in a function, then we won't be able to use the variable from another function; if we place it in a code file, other code files won't be able to access the variable.

Create a new project for this example. We'll use a variable called hidingVariable and set it in three ways: as a global variable in the main code file, as a local variable in an external file, and as a local variable in a function. The code is quite simple, and we just have to make sure we add the local keyword whenever we want the effect to be local and omit it if we want the variable's changes to transfer to other code files.

First create the global hidingVariable variable; then set its value to "global".

GameLoop/GameLoop_Local_Global/main.lua

```
-- Define a global variable called hidingVariable,
--    and set its value to "global"
print( "Setting the global hidingVariable to \"global\"" )
hidingVariable = "global"
print ( "the global hidingVariable = " .. hidingVariable )
```

Now create a new file and create a local hidingVariable variable. Set its value to "local".

GameLoop/GameLoop_Local_Global/hidingvariable.lua

```
-- Use a local variable called hidingVariable in this file
--    and set its value to "local"
print( "Setting the file's local hidingVariable to \"local\"" )
local hidingVariable = "local"
print( "In hidingVariable.lua, hidingVariable = " .. hidingVariable )
```

If you write a function and update a local instance of the variable within it, its changes will not affect the global variable's output.

GameLoop/GameLoop_Local_Global/main.lua
```
-- Create a function that uses a function-level hidingVariable
--     and set its value to "function"
-- Store a local variable
function checkHidingVariable( )
    print( "Setting the function's local hidingVariable to \"function\"" )
    local hidingVariable = "function"
    print( "In the function, hidingVariable = " .. hidingVariable )
end
```

Let's try an experiment and check whether Corona can access the variables. We'll add a few print() statements along the way and see how it affects the variable we can access. To run the code in hidingvariable.lua, you'll have to use a function called require(), which includes a different code file from the game. This will be really useful when we start making more complex games.

GameLoop/GameLoop_Local_Global/main.lua
```
-- Run the function and print the variable's value
checkHidingVariable( )
print( "After the function ends, the global " ..
    "hidingVariable is still = " .. hidingVariable )

-- Include the external file and print the value again
require( "hidingvariable" )
print( "After including the external file, the global " ..
    "hidingVariable is still = " .. hidingVariable )
```

As you can see in Figure 9, *Local and global variables*, on page 25, local variables within a function mean that we'll access that variable's value, and using them in external files means that we won't be able to read them.

It's good to keep this in mind if we are ever tempted to name local and global variables using the same names!

Tables and Loops

Sometimes we'll want to keep track of a list of related items. For example, if one of your games has ten or more enemies, it makes sense to store their properties in a single variable instead of hard-coding a variable for each of them. That's where tables come in handy. We can use a table to store a list of values (even of varying size) and access them using one common name.

Since we're using tables, we also need a way to access each of their values. We could do it manually, but it would be just as laborious as hard-coding one variable for each enemy in a game; it's just not practical. Instead, we can

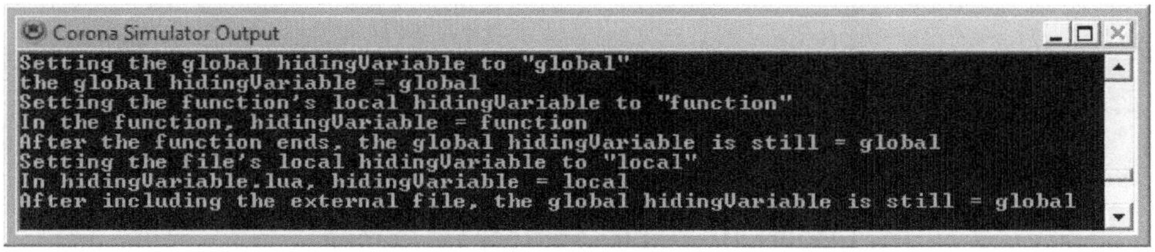

```
Corona Simulator Output
Setting the global hidingVariable to "global"
the global hidingVariable = global
Setting the function's local hidingVariable to "function"
In the function, hidingVariable = function
After the function ends, the global hidingVariable is still = global
Setting the file's local hidingVariable to "local"
In hidingVariable.lua, hidingVariable = local
After including the external file, the global hidingVariable is still = global
```

Figure 9—Local and global variables

use loops, which perform a function *n* times and just repeat the same task for each of our related variables. In the example of storing enemies, we can move them all easily by storing them in a table and looping through the table to call each enemy's move function. That's it. We write the code once and use it several times.

Let's use the print() function we've just learned and make Corona count from 1 to 5. In Lua, we use for and while to iterate through values. We could print 1 to 5 using a variable, but let's also define a *list*. Lists in Lua are like arrays in other languages; they store a set of related values. We store them using the curly brackets, as in variable = { }, and we can access an element like in many other languages using the square brackets, such as variable[position]. Lua's lists start their position counter at 1, so the first value will be at variable[1]. Other languages use 0 to access the first value in a list, so it's easy to forget this and get an out-of-range error.

In the following example, we'll store a list with the values from 1 to 5 and use an iterator variable called i to loop through the numbers. In each loop step, we'll use print() to output the list's value to the console. It's a very basic example, but it showcases most of the *traditional* programming concepts we'll need to code games: loops, lists, and displaying messages using the console.

GameLoop/GameLoop_Tables_Loops/main.lua
```lua
-- Define a number list
myNumberList = { 1, 2, 3, 4, 5 }

-- Loop through the list and print each number on the console
for i = 1, #myNumberList do
    print( myNumberList[ i ] )
end
```

This example was very easy, and you can see the output in the console (see Figure 10, *Tables and loops in Corona*, on page 26). It works with lists and loops exactly like we'll work in game programming.

Figure 10—Tables and loops in Corona

Most of the time, we'll use lists instead of variables because we'll have a varying number of enemies, bullets, or other game objects. We'll loop through them because we'll make them have similar behaviors. For example, bullets will all move in straight lines, so we can code movement once and apply it to all bullets using a loop.

Using Classes in Corona

If you've used other languages in the past, you'll certainly have heard of *classes*. If you haven't heard of them, don't worry. Classes are a tool to help programmers group similar elements in a program and set common variable names and functions for those classes. For example, if we're making a driving video game, we can make a Car class and code all the driving functions in it.

We're then able to use that Car class to create *instances*, or elements that use those functions and variables. We could create variables for a redCar, a slowCar, and an oldCar, using the Car class as our base. In each of these instances, we'd have to focus only on their speed and maneuverability instead of rewriting the movement functions again and again.

Choosing a Class System

Since Corona uses Lua, it doesn't really come with a fully featured class system. To be able to use classes, we can use a custom library that lets us repeat the same code and functions for some variables over and over again without having to repeat our code. We can write our own code to do this, we can search the Internet and choose our favorite Lua class system, or we can use the class.lua file from this chapter's code files.[1] In this book, we'll use class.lua from the code files in most of the chapters, so make sure to download it.

To choose a class system, we have to make sure that it's easy to use and that we can expand it to suit our needs. At this point, we don't need to know how the class system in the chapter's code files works; we need to know only how

---

1. Remember that you can download the book's code files from http://pragprog.com/book/ sdcorona/create-mobile-games-with-corona.

to use it. However, in case you're curious, here's a high-level summary: It's basically some functions that let us create a new class instance using a class's ClassName() function. Calling this will call its ClassName:new() function to create a new instance of the class object. We can use the self variable within class functions to access the instance. If you already feel comfortable using Lua, you can get more details about how this works Appendix 2, *Classes in Corona*, on page 221. Otherwise, let's stop talking about complex theories and try a few experiments to see how this really works.

Creating a New Class

Instead of focusing on the theory, let's try an example. We've used numbers and the Corona console's print() function, so let's write a MathsNumber class to perform a few operations for us. We'll use this class to store a list of numbers, a function to add a new number to the list, and another function to calculate the list's average.

In the class function we're using, we can create a new class by using the Class() command, so start by initializing the MathsNumber class. Also initialize the list of numbers, listOfNumbers, to keep track of all the numbers we've added so far.

GameLoop/GameLoop_Classes/main.lua

```lua
-- Create a new class
MathsNumber = Class( )

-- Initialize a list of numbers
listOfNumbers = { }
```

After creating the new class, move on to writing the constructor, or Class-Name:new(). First add the number to the list of numbers, and then calculate a few mathematical operations. Let's keep things simple at this point—print the number's square, its square root using math.sqrt(), and its cosine using math.cos().

GameLoop/GameLoop_Classes/main.lua

```lua
-- Create the MathsNumber constructor
function MathsNumber:new( number )
    -- Store the value as one of the instance's properties
    --   use "self" to access the instance's own variables
    self.value = number
    -- Print the number, its square, its square root, and its cosine
    print( "Number: "..number )
    print( "Square: "..(number * number) )
    print( "Square Root: ".. (math.sqrt(number)) )
    print( "Cosine: ".. (math.cos(number)) )
end
```

Call MathsNumber:new to add a new number to the list, and it will output the number, followed by its square, square root, and cosine.

Now that we have these functions, we can perform operations with the numbers we're adding to listOfNumbers in MathsNumber:new(). Since we want to calculate the average, create a new calculateAverage() function. Loop through the numbers and add them up, and then divide the total sum by the list size.

GameLoop/GameLoop_Classes/main.lua
```lua
-- Calculates the average of the list of numbers
function calculateAverage( )
    -- Initialize a variable to 0
    local total = 0
    -- Add each number from the list to the total
    for i = 1, #listOfNumbers do
        total = total + listOfNumbers[ i ].value
    end
    -- Divide the total by the number of numbers
    print( )
    print( "The sum is: " .. total )
    average = total / #listOfNumbers
    print( "The average is: "..average )
end
```

Now that we have the average calculating function, it's easy to add a few numbers to the list, such as 1, 3, 5, 7, and 9, by calling MathsNumber(), and then calculate the average of all five numbers.

GameLoop/GameLoop_Classes/main.lua
```lua
-- Create five instances of the class and add them to the list of numbers
listOfNumbers [ #listOfNumbers + 1 ] = MathsNumber(1)
listOfNumbers [ #listOfNumbers + 1 ] = MathsNumber(3)
listOfNumbers [ #listOfNumbers + 1 ] = MathsNumber(5)
listOfNumbers [ #listOfNumbers + 1 ] = MathsNumber(7)
listOfNumbers [ #listOfNumbers + 1 ] = MathsNumber(9)
-- Calculate the average
calculateAverage( )
```

When you run this program, you will see something similar to Figure 11, *Using classes in Corona*, on page 29. It first calculates the square, square root, and cosine for each of the numbers, and then it calculates the average.

This was a really easy example, but it'll be the base of most of our game-development code. The main difference is that we'll work with sprites and images instead of numbers—we're game developers, after all!

As you can see, classes save us time and energy by letting us reuse code. Even though using classes can seem daunting at first, we'll quickly get used to them. The easiest way to approach them is to think of common properties

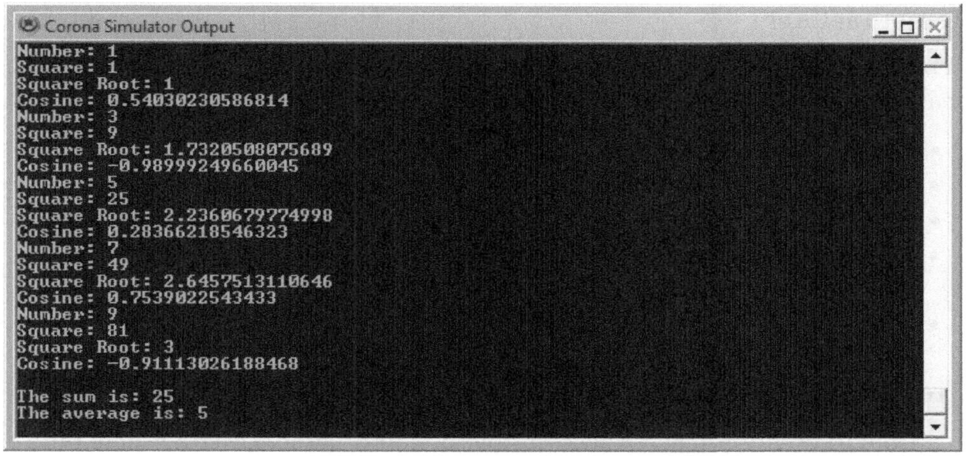

```
Corona Simulator Output                                    _ □ ×
Number: 1
Square: 1
Square Root: 1
Cosine: 0.54030230586814
Number: 3
Square: 9
Square Root: 1.7320508075689
Cosine: -0.98999249660045
Number: 5
Square: 25
Square Root: 2.2360679774998
Cosine: 0.28366218546323
Number: 7
Square: 49
Square Root: 2.6457513110646
Cosine: 0.7539022543433
Number: 9
Square: 81
Square Root: 3
Cosine: -0.91113026188468

The sum is: 25
The average is: 5
```

Figure 11—Using classes in Corona

we can easily see; there's no need to second-guess ourselves. In an avatar-dressing game, if we want to code shirts, pants, and socks, we can group them as clothes and write a clothes class to make our life easier.

2.3 Designing Our First Game: Planet Defender

Now that we've installed Corona and learned the basic programming vocabulary and techniques needed to develop games, it's time to start making a real game.

For our first project, we'll design a game that we can code and understand using the basic knowledge that we already have. We'll need to create and manage three main things.

- A way for the game to keep updating itself, frame after frame, in an endless loop that handles most of the game-related code (a game loop)

- A set of images to graphically represent the elements of the game (sprites)

- A few buttons and a start menu to enable the player to interact with the game (interactivity)

To make things easier on ourselves as beginners, we'll design a game with as little movement as possible—a space-themed game with enemy ships that fly in straight lines toward a planet at the bottom of the screen. The player will be in charge of defending the planet by destroying (tapping) the approaching ships. The game will end whenever an enemy ship reaches the planet.

Target Features

When designing a game, the best way to begin is by outlining a list of the features the game will have. For our first game, we'll need the following:

- A background image
- A properly positioned planet image
- Enemy ships that move toward the planet
- Functions to interpret and act on player input (screen taps) so that ships can be destroyed
- A score counter

2.4 Creating the Project

It's time to create a new project to hold our first game. Create a new multi-screen application. Rename the automatically generated scenetemplate.lua scene file to game.lua—we'll work only on the project's gameplay, so calling the code file game.lua makes it easier to recognize. It's important to change the scene names to something explicit because it makes coding much easier in the long run. Using scenetemplate.lua can be more comfortable now, but in five months' time we might not remember what the scene had, and we'll have to read it to know whether that's the file we want to update.

We also have to open main.lua to update the file we want to load first, because otherwise we'll get an error once the program attempts to open scenetemplate.lua. To update this, make sure that main.lua calls the scene name by using storyboard.gotoScene().

GameLoop/GameLoop/main.lua
```
-- Require the Storyboard API
local storyboard = require "storyboard"

-- load the game.lua scene
storyboard.gotoScene( "game" )
```

Now that the program will go directly to the game scene, it's time for us to start working on it.

Drawing the Background Image

Since it's a bit daunting to start using a new programming language without seeing results, let's begin by adding a background image to the game. As game developers, seeing images in our games is great because they let us see that the program isn't broken (or at least not completely). We'll sometimes have to make further checks to see whether the nonvisual code is working, but seeing images behave in the way we expect them to is usually a good sign.

We can draw an image on the stage by calling the display.newImage() function. Pass as a parameter the name of an image located in the game project folder, and Corona will load and display the image. To load an image called space_background.jpg, write display.newImage("space_background.jpg"). The function returns the image Corona has just loaded, so you'll usually want to store it as a local variable to be able to change its properties easily. You can save images in a folder to make your project folder neater, and then pass the relative path (for example, foldername/space_background.jpg) to this function.

When working with images, we can't just add them anywhere and hope they look good. In games, we usually work with many images, so we have to make sure each image is well-positioned. Also, when changing scenes, it's common to remove everything from the stage. To make it easier for us to access all objects on the stage, Corona has something called display *groups*. A group (or display group) in Corona is just like a folder on your PC— it helps you keep your images organized. Each scene automatically generated by Corona comes with a group variable called group where we can add our scene objects. We can use that whenever we work with images.

Figure 12—The game's background image

To add a display object to a group, call the group:insert() function, and the image will be added to the scene's main group. Now load a background image using display.newImage() and add it to the main scene group using group:insert().

GameLoop/GameLoop/game.lua
```
-- Load an image and add it to the scene's main group
local image = display.newImage( "images/space_background.jpg" )
group:insert( image )
```

If you compile the project now, you'll be able to see the image in action, as shown in Figure 12, *The game's background image*.

Right now, it doesn't move or do anything, but it's always nice to see that the previously empty stage is no longer empty.

2.5 Coding the Game Loop

Having images on the screen is great, but we need a way to regularly update them to create the illusions of motion and activity. Otherwise, players will be bored by bullets, enemies, and a player character that just sit there, motionless. In this game, we have to move enemy ships and get rid of dead units (the ones that have been tapped).

Adding an Event Listener

Corona divides every second into a fixed number of up to sixty *frames*, which is the number of times that the stage is rendered and shown to the user. We can ask the program to call a function of our choosing whenever it's time for a new frame to appear. We tell Corona to do this using an *event listener* called enterFrame.

An event listener is like a little spy in Corona programs that will call a function for us (whichever function we ask it to call) whenever a specific event happens. In the case of the enterFrame listener, the event is the start of a new frame. Corona has other listeners that can call a function each time an animation changes, when a sound ends, or even when the player taps the screen. We ask an event listener to do these things for us by calling the addEventListener() function. If we want an event listener to focus on just one object, we'll call object:addEventListener(), but when we want to track a generic event such as when the stage moves to the next frame, we'll use Runtime:addEventListener(), which assigns the listener to the game's running environment in general.

Many game developers call their frame-update functions either tick() or enter-Frame(). We'll use tick() because it's easier to write and reminds us that time is passing with each update. We'll use the tick() name for all of our frame-update functions throughout the book, but remember that you can name the function in any way you like and it will still be called as long as you pass its name to the addEventListener() function along with "enterFrame".

Now write an empty tick() function to later call it through an enterFrame event listener.

GameLoop/GameLoop/game.lua
```
-- A placeholder for the tick function
--  Called every frame
function tick( )
    -- Here we'll add the code that needs to be executed each frame
end
```

Now that we know the type of event we'll add (enterFrame), the function we need to call to set up the event listener (Runtime:addEventListener()), and the function we want the event listener to call (tick()), add the event listener to the enterScene() function to call tick() sixty times per second. Remember that Corona generated enterScene() automatically when we created a new storyboard project and that the function is called as soon as the program enters the scene.

GameLoop/GameLoop/game.lua

```
-- Add an event listener
-- This will call the tick function each frame:
Runtime:addEventListener( "enterFrame", tick )
```

This enterFrame event listener is like a little CIA agent who will watch the game and call the tick() function, which is like the headquarters, every time the program enters a new frame. All we have to do now is add code to the tick() function to update all of the game's objects, doing whatever needs to be done in each frame to make this program behave like a game.

Adding EnterFrame Listeners to Objects

Corona lets us add event listeners to actual game objects. This means we can keep track of when the player touches an object in the game and if two objects collide with each other. We can also add an enterFrame event listener to game objects such as sprites, which you'll learn about in Chapter 3, *Sprites and Movement*, on page 37. However, if we add event listeners to objects that can be removed from the game, we need to make sure we also call the removeEventListener() function to remove the listeners. Otherwise, we might not clear it out properly, and it might be called for as long as the app remains active.

To avoid this, it's a good idea to avoid enterFrame events, consolidate actions in the game tick(), and make sure that we call relevant update functions for each of the objects on the stage. That way, the only time we'll have to remove an enterFrame event listener is if we ever leave the game scene. This also saves Corona from keeping track of lots of event listeners; if we're routinely tracking a series of recurrent events for lots of objects, then we can also consolidate them into a single event and loop through affected objects.

Updating the Game

Now we have a game that calls the tick() function regularly, but it doesn't actually do anything that a player can see yet because we haven't provided any instructions to Corona in the tick() function. Generally speaking, each time through tick() we'll check to see whether we need to add new objects (like enemy ships or bullets) to the game and whether a player has tapped an existing object, and we'll need to update all of the existing objects (move enemy ships, remove a ship that has been tapped, and so on).

The easiest way to structure a game loop is to make a mental list of all the objects in the game and then add a function call to them in the tick() function that updates each of them appropriately (whatever that may mean) in each frame. Planet Defender is a simple game, so the only objects that we need to update are the enemy ships. We'll also have to occasionally add new ships to the game, which adds a little wrinkle, but there's no "player ship" object in this game, or any other complications for the time being.

Structuring the Game Loop

Now that we've decided the tick() function will need to create enemy ships and update them as time passes, we can write a basic set of instructions using placeholder function calls for each of the actions we plan to add. This means we'll call the functions we need to have (as though we'd already written them), and then we can actually create each of the needed functions afterward. This makes it easy to have a manageable big-picture view of what we're doing and also keeps our tick() function clean and simple, even in complex games with lots and lots of updates and instructions. A game's tick() function is like its brain, so it's a good idea to keep it neat and organized so that it's easy to maintain and update the game as needed.

Let's start by adding placeholder calls to the tick() function. Add calls to functions named updateEnemies() and addEnemies(). updateEnemies() will update the enemy ships, and addEnemies() will add new enemies to the game.

GameLoop/GameLoop/game.lua

```lua
-- The tick function that will get called each frame
function tick( )
    -- Call several functions to update our game
    updateEnemies( )
    addEnemies( )
end
```

At this point, the game will try to call both of those functions each frame. Since we haven't written these yet, if we try to run the game, Corona will complain because it can't find the functions. Let's begin to fix this by writing an updateEnemies() function just before the createScene() function. This function needs to update the enemy ship positions on the screen to create the illusion of movement as time passes and to remove any ships that need to be removed. Since we haven't yet covered how to add ships, write a short comment describing what we want the function to do, and we'll get around to the actual code in in the next chapter. Also, print a short Enemies updated message on the console (this message will be printed once each frame) to see that the tick function is really being called.

GameLoop/GameLoop/game.lua

```lua
-- This function will update our enemies each frame
function updateEnemies( )
    print( "Enemies updated" )
end
```

Now write the addEnemies() function. We'll also put off the real work that goes into this function for now, so print another message saying Enemies added each time this function gets called.

Once you add this, running the code in the simulator should result in alternating messages on the console saying that the enemies have been updated and added, churning out very quickly. If these messages don't appear, it means that something (calls to a function, an event listener, and so on) is probably missing or mistyped. This simple debugging technique illustrates why the print() function is so useful.

You can also use a debugger from some of the integrated development environments Appendix 1, *Corona Resources*, on page 215.

GameLoop/GameLoop/game.lua
```
-- This function is called each frame and will add enemies to the game
function addEnemies( )
    print( "Enemies added" )
end
```

We've written the most basic game loop we can think of, yet it's a good way to see how to update games. This code is ready to be turned into something playable with the addition of a bit more code. We can add anything we want to the tick() function, or to any functions that it calls, and all of the instructions in them will be carried out each time Corona enters a new frame.

Configuring the Frame Rate

The game loop function is ready to do our bidding with each tick of Corona's clock, but we might want more or fewer ticks every second depending on whether we're coding fast-paced action or very slow-moving games. We can set the number of frames per second (FPS) that will occur in the game by updating the program's build.settings configuration file and assigning a value to the fps variable. When we set this variable to either 30 or 60 (the two choices that Corona accepts), the app will enter a new frame either thirty or sixty times per second, respectively.

GameLoop/GameLoop/build.settings
```
-- Change our game's frame rate to 30 or 60 (30 in this case)
fps = 30,
```

For this game, we'll keep the value at 30, which is the default value if we don't change anything. In any case, it's a good idea to test both speeds to see the difference in a game.

2.6 What We Covered

In this chapter, we covered how to create a game loop and event listeners, which are the fundamental frameworks that we'll use to build all of the games in this book. We saw how a series of functions called from the game loop come together into something that players experience as a game. We created a game project for our first game, Planet Defender, and wrote placeholder functions for enemy-ship creation and updates. In the next chapter, we'll build on this chapter's work, adding spaceships and other things that will begin to turn our project into an entertaining game.

CHAPTER 3

Sprites and Movement

Now that we have a game loop working, we can start to add images to make our app look more like a real game.

3.1 What You'll Learn

In this chapter, we'll continue working on the Planet Defender app. We'll do the following:

- Learn how to load and display images and animations in games
- Write a game object class to write all the ship movement and image-creation functions
- Add spaceships that move from the screen borders toward the planet

By the end of the chapter, our app will look like the image shown earlier.

3.2 Displaying Images

We have already discussed how to load an image and display it on the screen. However, most of the games we'll make will need to load many more images. Corona can load an image called a *texture atlas* that contains all the images we'll need for a game (or a big fraction of them). These texture atlases are made of all the different images, and they're usually accompanied by a code file that tells Corona where to find each image.

We don't have to worry about making these files manually—it would be crazy to keep track of all the different pixels. Programs like TexturePacker automatically combine our individual images to create a Corona-compatible texture atlas.[1]

---

1. You can get TexturePacker from http://www.codeandweb.com/texturepacker.

Let's use texture atlases to load and display a set of images. I've saved us the work of either manually writing the code or using one of the image-packing programs, and I've created shipsprites.lua using TexturePacker. If you use one of these tools, you just have to open it and drag the images you'll use in the game, and the program will combine them and output a code file with the sprite definitions. The file in this chapter's code files is ready to be used, and we can jump directly into writing real code instead of worrying about making our own image sheets.

In Corona, we create image sheets from texture atlases by calling the graphics.newImageSheet() function. We have to pass the image filename as the first parameter and pass a list of options as the second parameter. The image sheet uses a texture-atlas image and a list of image coordinates to know where to find each image.

We have many ways of passing the options parameter: a simple mode for images that have the same width and height, a complex mode for images of different sizes, and an old-style mode that is compatible with previous versions of Corona. We're learning new content, so we can forget about the old style and focus on simple and complex modes.

Simple Image Sheets

The easiest image sheets all use the same width and height. This is called the simple mode of using texture atlases. The options variable we'll pass will be a table with three to five variables. We have to pass the pixel width and height of one image frame and pass the total number of frames (numFrames). We can also pass two extra variables called sheetContentWidth and sheetContentHeight, which are useful in case we have to use Retina graphics.

Call the graphics.newImageSheet() function for a texture atlas found at myImage-Sheet.png with two frames of 50×100 pixels in size.

SpritesExamples/Buttons/main.lua
```
-- Store the options to use images of constant size
-- (This is nice for buttons and menus)
local spriteOptions = {
    -- Define the number of frames and image sizes
    numFrames = 2,
    width = 80,
    height = 40
}

-- Create the image sheet
local imageSheet = graphics.newImageSheet( "myImageSheet.png",
    spriteOptions )
```

As you can see, it's really easy to create simple sprite sheets. This sprite mode is great if all your images are the same size. In that case, you don't need to specify the width, height, and position of each image because you'd have to keep repeating the same numbers again and again.

Complex Image Sheets

In most games, we'll end up using a varied mixture of images to display characters, objects, backgrounds, and buildings, so images won't all be the same size. This means we won't be able to use the simple image-sheet definition mode, and we'll have to pass individual widths, heights, and positions for each of the images in the texture atlases. These are called *complex* image sheets.

Call graphics.newImageSheet() and pass the options as a table with each frame's x and y coordinates and width and height. For this example, create the same image sheet as before, but define the details (50×100, with two frames) explicitly for each frame.

SpritesExamples/Smileys/main.lua

```lua
-- Store the options for two different images
local spriteOptions = { -- array of tables representing each frame (required)
frames =
{
    -- Store the image sizes in a frames list
    frames =
        {
            name = "smile",
            x = 0,
            y = 0,
            width = 32,
            height = 32
        },
        {
            name = "frown",
            x = 32,
            y = 0,
            width = 32,
            height = 32
        },
    },
}

-- Create the image sheet
local complexImageSheet = graphics.newImageSheet( "myImageSheet.png",
    spriteOptions )
```

This step is very laborious, and making a silly mistake when setting an image's coordinates can lead to unexpected results—we could accidentally cut a character in half!

Luckily for us, there are several programs, such as TexturePacker, that will automatically create an image-sheet definition file. We'll only have to open them, drag the images we want to add to the file, and export the file.

Even if you prefer not to use any commercial programs, it's a good idea to write a macro or another system to create Corona image-sheet files. Once our games start becoming complex, it's crazy to combine image sheets manually.

Using TexturePacker Image Sheets

TexturePacker is one of the programs that automatically generates image-sheet data, and it allows you to export image data to many popular formats used to develop games with other engines, such as Unity and cocos2D. You can use any program you want—or write the data yourself—but I've used this program to create the image-atlas definitions in the book's accompanying code. Let's review how these data files work so that we're able to call them throughout the remainder of the book.

Whenever you export an image file in TexturePacker, you get a Lua file with all the image coordinates and their names. This file will have two functions that will help us create our images: getSheet() and getFrameIndex(). We'll use getSheet() to get the image data needed to call graphics.newImageSheet(). We'll use getFrameIndex() to get the frame number for any of our images. That way, we can use a name (instead of numbers) to refer to images. Otherwise, the numbers can get confusing once our programs use many different images.

Displaying an Image

Once we've created an image sheet, we can go back to Corona's application programming interface (API) functions and add images to our game. To display static images from the set of images we've defined in the image atlas, call display.newImage(). Pass the image sheet and frame number as parameters.

SpritesExamples/Smileys/main.lua
```lua
-- Display the image on the left of our image sheet
local myImage = display.newImage( complexImageSheet, 1 )
```

We might also want to display the image using a different size. We'll be able to call display.newImageRect() and pass the image sheet, frame number, width, and height. This is useful if we want to resize one of our images, such as when drawing a smaller health bar when a character is hurt.

SpritesExamples/Smileys/main.lua

```
-- Get a 16x16 smiley face using newImageRect
--    so that proper resolutions are picked depending on the device
local topLeftImage = display.newImageRect( complexImageSheet, 1, 16, 16 )
```

Once we've created our images and added them to the stage, it's always a good idea to add them to a *group*. Groups in Corona are like layers: each group can hold other groups, and images in the top group will appear above images in the background. We usually do that by calling the display.newGroup() function to create a group and using the group:insert() function to add an object to the group.

Now create a group and store it in a variable called myGroup. Add the image called myImage to it.

SpritesExamples/Smileys/main.lua

```
-- Create a new group and insert myImage
local myGroup = display.newGroup( )
myGroup:insert( myImage )
```

If we always follow this group-adding method whenever we add objects to our games, we'll be able to avoid accidents such as displaying new units on top of explosions instead of making explosions appear on the foreground.

3.3 Animated Sprites

So far, we've used only static images in Corona. Those are great for traditional apps, but since we're making games, we need to use animations too. In our games, we'll work with game objects just like the images we've used so far, but these objects will have functions to tell them what animation to play or when to stop. In game development, we call these animated images *sprites*.

Corona comes with a Sprite API that can be used by calling display.newSprite(). We have to pass the image sheet we're using for our app and a sequenceData list holding the sprite's animations as parameters. This sounds a bit complicated as a wall of text, so let's try an example to see how it works.

We'll continue using the imageSheet we created in the previous example, so at this point we've already loaded the image and have our program ready to start using sprites.

Define a sequenceData table for one animation called "walking" (don't forget to include the quotes; they are necessary!). This animation starts in the image sheet's first frame and lasts for two frames. Define the sequenceData's name, start frame, and frame count using the values shown in the following example. Then call display.newSprite() to create a sprite using this animation.

SpritesExamples/Walking/main.lua
```lua
-- Define the sprite's sequence data
--    (the frames and animations we'll work with)
local sequenceData = {
    -- Set the name, a starting frame, and the number of frames
    name = "walking",
    start = 1,
    count = 4,
    time = 800
}

-- Add a sprite using newSprite
local mySprite = display.newSprite( imageSheet, sequenceData )

-- Set the walking animation
mySprite:setSequence( "walking" )
mySprite:play( )
```

The sequenceData list might look a bit complicated for now, but it contains only the animation data. There are two main ways to tell Corona the animations we want it to display, depending on whether we've passed the animation sequences to the image sheet in order. If we have, we can pass the start frame and total number of frames; otherwise, we'll have to manually pass the different frame numbers.

Animations with Consecutive Frames

The easiest way to animate a sprite is to use consecutive frames from the image-data file. This means it's a good idea to group image coordinates and set them consecutively to avoid having to name the frames. If the frames are consecutive, we can set start and count variables in the sequenceData table. Corona will automatically get count frames from the image-data table, starting in the start position. We also need to pass a variable with the animation name, which is the string we'll use if we want to play the animation in the future.

Now update the previous code to use getFrameIndex() to get the starting frame ID.

SpritesExamples/TexturePacker/main.lua
```lua
-- Define an animation sequence using TexturePacker files
local sequenceData = {
    -- Set the name, a starting frame, and the number of frames
    name = "walking",
    start = sheetInfo:getFrameIndex( "walk_sprite0001" ),
    time = 600,
    count = 4
}
-- Add a sprite using newSprite
local mySprite = display.newSprite( imageSheet, sequenceData )
```

Aside from these parameters, we can pass other optional parameters, such as the time between frames; the loopCount, which is the number of loops before stopping the animation; and the loopDirection, which can be either forward or bounce and which determines whether the animation loops normally or loops backward in even loops.

Animations with Nonconsecutive Frames

We can create animations by passing a table with the frame order that we want our animations to follow. This method is useful if we want to repeat some frames more than once and avoid repeating the frame image in the atlas. If we use repeated frames in many of our games' animations, we can use a lot of extra space if we add them as individual images. Using animations with nonconsecutive frames lets us define animations without worrying about image-file size constraints.

To use nonconsecutive frames, instead of passing start and count variables in the sequenceData table, we can pass a list of frames. For example, if our frames are 1, 2, 3, 4, pass frames = { 1, 2, 3, 4 }.

Now add a sprite with an animation loop of 1, 3.

SpritesExamples/NonConsecutiveFrames/main.lua
```lua
-- Define an animation sequence using non-consecutive frames
local sequenceData = {
    -- Set the name and frames in the animation
    name = "walking",
    frames = { 1, 3 },
    time = 600
}
-- Add a sprite using newSprite
local mySprite = display.newSprite( imageSheet, sequenceData )
```

In some old-school role-playing games, this animation sequence can be a walk loop for one of the characters, and it helps us save one frame per animation. Imagine that we used ten characters with four walk directions in a game: defining animations through nonconsecutive frames would allow us to avoid saving forty repeated images. This number can be a lot higher for more complex games.

Using Multiple Animations

So far, we've learned how to create a new sprite and display one animation. However, in many games we will want to animate our units with several different loops. For instance, a character in a platform game will usually need running and jumping animation. Since both actions are exclusive, we can't create one animation that includes both of them. Corona lets us define multiple animations if we pass a list of animation data like the consecutive or nonconsecutive animations we've just done.

Now define a sprite with a sequenceData composed of two animations. Write the first animation by passing the value "static" so that it has one frame and starts at frame 1. The second animation can be name = "moving", with four frames in the order 1, 2, 3, 4.

SpritesExamples/TwoAnimations/main.lua
```lua
-- Define multiple animations
local sequenceData = {
    -- Sequence 1
    {
        name = "static",
        start = 1,
        count = 1
    },
    -- Sequence 2
    {
        name = "moving",
        frames = { 1, 2, 3, 4 },
        time = 800
    }
}
-- Add a sprite using newSprite
local mySprite = display.newSprite( imageSheet, sequenceData )
```

In this example, our sprite has two animations: static and moving. We can play one of the animations by using the setSequence() function and passing one of these names as its parameter.

SpritesExamples/TwoAnimations/main.lua
```lua
-- Set the walking animation
mySprite:setSequence( "moving" )
mySprite:play( )
```

At this point, the program runs and loads and displays the moving animation. We are able to pause an animation by calling its pause() function, but we'll usually call it less often in games.

Removing a Sprite

Even though modern mobile devices are much more powerful than they used to be, it's always a good idea to clean up after we've used graphic resources that we no longer need. We can remove a sprite instance by calling its removeSelf() function. We also have to update all references to the sprite instance to nil. In this case, we have to update only one.

SpritesExamples/RemoveSprite/main.lua

```
-- Remove the sprite
mySprite:removeSelf()
mySprite = nil
```

As you can see in the previous code, it's easy to ensure that our sprites are removed. It keeps the program clean, and users won't complain that we're draining their phones' battery life. Writing these functions is annoying, because we have to write more than one. The easiest way to call sprite-deletion functions is to write a base sprite class that includes the creation and removal functions and just inherit from it for each of our game objects. We'll work on these functions throughout the rest of the chapter.

3.4 Handling Many Images

Now that we know how to load and animate a single image, we're ready to make really simple apps. It would be tiresome to write the same code over and over again for each sprite we added to the screen. To avoid this, we'll group our sprites with the same code using a common code file. Remember how we used a simple class in *Using Classes in Corona*, on page 26? Now, we'll use a class to hold sprite information so that we can focus on coding gameplay instead of coding sprites again and again. From this point on, we'll continue working on Planet Defender, the game we started in the previous chapter.

To create a class, start by creating a new file called gamesprite.lua. We can call our custom sprite class GameSprite because Corona already uses the sprite class name. In this file, we'll add all our sprite-related functions to add sprites to the stage, move them, and remove them from the screen. That way, we'll *encapsulate*, or combine into a comfortable class, all of Corona's functions. Using a custom sprite class will make our lives much easier because we'll be able to avoid repeating code in all the game objects that use sprites.

Our class will need functions or code to do the following:

- Create a new sprite and add it to a Corona group so that we can call one function to create a sprite

- Set a sprite's animation and change it

- Move a sprite to another location on the screen so that we don't have to keep updating its x and y positions

- Let us inherit all the functions from a new game object class so that we can customize our code once we start adding different objects to our games

Creating a Sprite Data File

The first step we'll take will be to write a sprite data file for the sprites we'll use in our game. We already have our image-data file, and the sprite data file will simply use our images to store the animations. We'll use those variables and the getFrameIndex() function to retrieve the correct frames for our animation. Let's try an example using the walking and idle animations we used earlier in this chapter. We'll store the sequenceData, either as a variable or as a function, so that we can access it from our main code files.

```lua
SpritesAndMovement/spriteanims.lua
spriteSequences.spaceshipSequence = {
    {
        name = SPR_SHIP,
        start = spritedata:getFrameIndex( SPR_SHIP ),
        count = 1
    }
}
```

From now on, we'll require() our sprite data file from the main code file to access the sequence data we've defined. It's always a good idea to keep our data files away from the actual game logic. Otherwise, the files get too long, and our programs can become very messy and difficult to update and understand.

Initializing and Removing the Sprite

Since we know how to initialize sprites, we can write the sprite-creation code in a function called initSprite(). Call display.newSprite() to create a new sprite instance, and store it in a spriteInstance variable. Since our class is going to be as generic as possible, create the sprite using the name we'll receive as a parameter. Use the sprite data file we just created to retrieve the details from this sprite name.

```lua
SpritesAndMovement/gamesprite.lua
-- Initialize the sprite using the spriteData for spriteName
function GameSprite:initSprite( sequence )
    self.spriteInstance = display.newSprite( imageSheet,
        sequence )
    -- Store the instance in the sprite
    self.spriteInstance.object = self
end
```

To remove the sprite, write a removeMe() function, and use it to call the two functions that remove sprites in Corona: removeSelf() and display.remove(). Update the spriteInstance variable to set it to nil so that we don't accidentally cause confusion for any of Corona's garbage-collection methods.

```
SpritesAndMovement/gamesprite.lua
function GameSprite:removeSprite( )
    self.spriteInstance:removeSelf( )
    self.spriteInstance = nil
end
```

From now on, we'll call the initSprite() and removeMe() functions from the game object classes, as long as they inherit from the GameSprite class.

Controlling Animations

Since we've stored the sprite instance in the self.spriteInstance variable, we'll be able to change the animation by calling its setSequence() function.

```
SpritesAndMovement/gamesprite.lua
-- Change the animation to animName and start playing
function GameSprite:changeAnimation( animName )
    self.spriteInstance:setSequence( animName )
    self.spriteInstance:play( )
end
```

Passing a string to indicate the animation we want to play is a bit messy (and we can accidentally mistype the animation name), so it's a good idea to use a variable instead. In this book, we'll usually save animation names as variables in an external code file so that we can access them just by requiring the file.

Updating the Sprite's Position

Apart from changing the sprite's animation, we'll have to update its position. In games, we'll want to either move an object to a specific location or move it a certain distance away from its current position. In the first movement type, we don't need to take its location into account, but in the other one, we do. This means it is much easier to write two separate functions to move a sprite: moveTo() and move(). The first one will translocate the sprite, and the second one will just move it in the direction we pass as a parameter.

Let's start by writing the moveTo() function to translocate the sprite. Update the spriteInstance's coordinates and set them to the values we receive as parameters. Since we're using a class in this example, we'll access spriteInstance from the self variable of the class instance.

```
SpritesAndMovement/gamesprite.lua
-- Translocate to posX, posY
function GameSprite:moveTo( posX, posY )
    self.spriteInstance.x = posX
    self.spriteInstance.y = posY
end
```

The move() method will be a bit more complex because we have to update the position. Instead of just setting the x and y coordinates, add the new values to the existing values.

SpritesAndMovement/gamesprite.lua
```lua
-- Move distanceX and distanceY
function GameSprite:move( distanceX, distanceY )
    self.spriteInstance.x = self.spriteInstance.x + distanceX
    self.spriteInstance.y = self.spriteInstance.y + distanceY
end
```

With these two functions, we can move sprites around the screen without worrying about writing all the movement code over and over again.

Adding the Sprite to the Stage

Like we've said a couple of times before, since Corona works with groups that function like layers, it's always a good idea to add all game objects to one or several groups. That way, we avoid piling up our objects by order of appearance. Instead, groups let us divide the scene into display layers.

To make our lives easier, we'll always pass an object's group whenever we call its constructor so that we can add the object to the group from the base sprite class.

Since we have to initialize the sprite and add it to a group from the beginning, we can create an initialise() function to call initSprite() and then add the newly created sprite to its group.

SpritesAndMovement/gamesprite.lua
```lua
-- Initialize the sprite and add it to the group
function GameSprite:initialize( sequence, group )
    self:initSprite( sequence )

    -- Only add it to the group if it is not nil
    if group ~= nil then
        group:insert( self.spriteInstance )
    end
end
```

That's it! Our GameSprite is now ready. We'll be able to inherit from it by calling class(GameSprite) whenever we create a new class that uses sprites.

3.5 Moving Images

Since we designed our sprite code to be reusable and expandable, we can expand our sprite class and add a movement function. Sprites on the stage won't move in the same way, so we'll create a new class and inherit from the

GameSprite class. This means that in the new class we'll be able to write code that won't change every other GameSprite instance. Since we're coding a space game, let's call our new class Spaceship.

Create the class and add a constructor where we'll set the sprite at a random position 400 pixels away from the center of the screen's lower bound. Call the initSprite() function from the constructor by passing both the group and the sprite name to initialize the sprite's animation. In this case, set the animation name using a string to make the process easier to understand (however, generally it's preferable to use a variable instead of a hard-coded string, because it will stop us from making typos).

SpritesAndMovement/spaceship.lua
```lua
-- Define a new Spaceship class
Spaceship = Class( GameSprite )

-- Create a new spaceship sprite
function Spaceship:new( group )
    -- Initialize the Spaceship sprite
    self:initialize( spriteAnims.spaceshipSequence, group )

    -- Set the start coordinates and rotation
    local rot = math.pi * ( -0.4 + math.random( 8 ) / 10 )
    local dx = SHIP_DIST * math.sin( rot )
    local dy = - SHIP_DIST * math.cos( rot )
    local x = PLANET_X + dx
    local y = PLANET_Y + dy
    local rot = 90 + math.atan2( dy, dx ) * 180 / math.pi
    self.spriteInstance.rotation = rot
    self:moveTo( x, y )

    -- Set the speed
    self.speed = 1 + math.random(3)
end
```

Now create a new instance of the class called spaceshipSprite to see how it behaves. To create an instance, call spaceship:new().

SpritesAndMovement/game.lua
```lua
-- Create a new spaceship instance
spaceshipSprite = Spaceship( )
```

We're using the code we started writing in the previous chapter, so Corona's enterFrame() events trigger our game loop's tick function. This means that we can call the update() function for the Spaceship class.

SpritesAndMovement/game.lua
```lua
-- Update the spaceship instance
spaceshipSprite:update( )
```

Now add some simple movement code to the GameSprite:update() method so that we can see how moving sprites works. We want enemies to move toward the planet to attack it, so we'll add movement code in here. For now, write an empty update() function.

SpritesAndMovement/spaceship.lua
```lua
-- Spaceship update function
--    (called each frame)
function Spaceship:update( )
    -- Ship movement goes here
end
```

Since we'll write the ship-updating code in its update() function, we'll be able to make all the other sprites move the same way just by calling the method for each of them. We haven't set the target coordinates yet, so store two variables called PLANET_X and PLANET_Y in a file called globals.lua so that we can quickly change the game's settings. Since we're setting them as global variables that should remain constant, using capital letters for the variable names reminds us that we're not supposed to change them.

SpritesAndMovement/globals.lua
```lua
-- The planet's coordinates
PLANET_X = 160
PLANET_Y = 480
```

After setting the target coordinates, we can calculate the distance difference between the sprite and its target position to move the spaceship in the update() function. Create two variables called dx and dy to get the x and y differences. Once you have those, calculate the hypotenuse by calculating dx * dx + dy * dy and taking the square root of the result. The sprite will move using a proportion: it will move more in the x direction with high dx values, and it will move less with low dx values.

If you enjoy math, you've probably guessed that we're going to move the ship using x = x + speed * dx / hyp. Now that we're at it, we can also rotate the spaceship using the sprite instance's rotation property so that it faces the direction in which the ship is moving.

SpritesAndMovement/spaceship.lua
```lua
-- Calculate the distance to the planet
local dx = PLANET_X - self.spriteInstance.x
local dy = PLANET_Y - self.spriteInstance.y
local hyp = dx * dx + dy * dy

    -- Move the sprite
    hyp = math.sqrt( hyp )
    self:move( self.speed * dx / hyp, self.speed * dy / hyp )
```

Finally, we'll have to make sure the hypotenuse is positive to avoid dividing by zero. Since the sprite is moving toward the center, it might end up with x and y exactly equal to the planet's x and y coordinates. Right now, we're not removing ships that attack the planet, so we could get errors linked to dividing by zero. Instead of checking that the hypotenuse is positive, check whether it's bigger than the planet's radius and call move() only if it is not. This will make ships stop as soon as they reach the planet.

SpritesAndMovement/spaceship.lua

```
-- Move the sprite only if the ship is not on the planet
if hyp > 2500 then
    -- Move the sprite
    hyp = math.sqrt( hyp )
    self:move( self.speed * dx / hyp, self.speed * dy / hyp )
end
```

Now that we've updated the tick() function and written the GameSprite:update method, our sprite will move toward the planet and stop as soon as it reaches the planet. Since our code is fully functional, we can compile the program and test whether everything is working properly and the ship is visible and moves toward the planet. It should look something like the following figure.

It's fun to run the program multiple times because the spaceship will appear at a different location each time the program loads.

3.6 Adding Spaceships to the Game

At this point, we've coded all the functions and classes we'll need to display a ship moving toward the planet. Since we've coded everything using classes, we can add multiple Spaceship instances to the stage. We'll create a list to keep track of the ships we have on the screen, and we'll update the tick() function so that it loops through the list instead of updating only one variable.

First we'll use a list of ships instead of using the ship variable to store the class instance. Remember that these variables are not equal

Figure 15—Lone invader

to the spaceships group; the lists are useful for us to loop through the instances, and the group holds the actual sprites. We can also access the spaceships group's elements by looping through the spaceships[i] variables. However, once we start adding other object types, such as bullets, to our games, it will be much easier to store a different list for each object type instead of looping through all the objects and checking the object type during the loop.

Define ships as an empty list by using curly brackets—{ and }.

SpritesAndMovementShips/game.lua
```
local ships = { }
```

Once our groups are ready, we'll update the tick() function to add enemies. We can add spaceships every three seconds by keeping track of the number of frames that have passed. Create a frame-delay counter called nextEnemy, and set it to 180, which is three times the game's frame rate.

Subtract one number from the counter in each frame. Once the counter reaches zero, call the Spaceship constructor and add the new ship to the list of ships.

SpritesAndMovementShips/game.lua
```
-- Add a new enemy every 3 seconds
nextEnemy = nextEnemy - 1
if nextEnemy < 0 then
    -- 3 seconds have passed, so create a new ship
    local newShip = Spaceship( )
    ships[ #ships + 1 ] = newShip

    -- Reset the enemy counter
    nextEnemy = 90
end
```

We have to loop through the list of enemies and call their update() functions to move the ships. Loop backward from the last element to the first instead of looping forward so that if we remove any enemies from the list in the middle of the loop, we don't have to update our loop variable.

SpritesAndMovementShips/game.lua
```
-- Loop through each of the enemies and update them
for i = #ships, 1, -1 do
    ships[ i ]:update( )
end
```

At this point, our app is starting to look like a real game (see Figure 16, *We're being invaded!*, on page 53). A new spaceship appears every three seconds at a random location outside the stage bounds, and it starts moving toward the planet. Once a ship reaches the planet, it stops moving. We'll have to remove it at that point and subtract life from the player, but we'll do that after we talk about user input in Chapter 4, *Input and Menus*, on page 55.

Since we created a class that takes care of most of the spaceship logic for us, this step has been much easier than explicitly writing the movement updates here. Another good aspect of storing the code in a spaceship class is that we can reuse these classes in the future if we want to add similar units to other games.

3.7 Exercise: Modifying the Game

Now that we've finished the chapter, here is an example of something we can change to improve this game.

Changing the Spaceship Image

Let's focus on an easy exercise and update our current code so that our spaceship uses a different image. To update the image, you'll have to change the image definitions in the ship-

Figure 16—We're being invaded!

sprites.lua file and make sure that they are adjusted to a new image. You can either generate the new images manually or use a program to do so automatically.

3.8 What We Covered

In this chapter, we discussed all we need to know about sprites and animation, and we were able to use these concepts to add units to our game. In the next chapter, we'll add menus to the start of the game. We'll also talk about buttons and, finally, add a way for players to destroy the invading hordes of enemy ships or face the destruction of their planet.

CHAPTER 4

Input and Menus

Even though our app showcases moving sprites and a background and has a general game feel to it, we haven't really added anything for players to do. It's time for us to add some interactivity.

4.1 What You'll Learn

In this chapter, we'll focus on completing the game we've worked on throughout the previous two chapters. We'll do the following:

- Add touch-based input to ships
- Remove ships that the players has tapped
- Add buttons and a main menu
- Finish our game by adding a life counter

Since this chapter builds completely upon the previous two chapters, make sure you have the chapter codes and are at least somewhat familiar with what we coded. Don't worry if you're a confident coder and have opted to skip the previous chapters; part of the game-programming process is to build upon existing programs or codes, so this chapter will be good practice in that regard. By the end of the chapter, our app will look like the image here.

4.2 Touch-Based Input

Touch-based input is almost a standard input method for mobile games, so this is a good topic to start learning about interactivity in Corona. You'll learn how to add touch event listeners, which are in charge of calling functions when the user taps an in-game object. This will make our spaceships interactive, and we'll delete any enemy ships whenever the player taps them.

To add a touch event listener, we'll add the listener when we create the ships. That listener will call a function whenever the user taps an object's area, and we'll use it to mark the ships as inactive. We'll also update the main game loop so that it removes inactive ships or those that reach the planet.

For this exercise, use a variable to mark it as not alive, such as isAlive. It'll be set to true by default, and we'll mark it as false if we want to delete that ship. Add it first to the constructor.

InputAndMenus/spaceship.lua
```lua
self.isAlive = true
self.wasKilled = nil
```

Start by updating the enemy-creation code in the tick() function. Instead of adding only the ships, add a touch listener to the ship object. You can add touch listeners in Corona using the addEventListener() function. You have to pass the listener type (in this case, touch) and the function that will be triggered (use a placeholder function called tappedShip()). We can do this by writing a single line of code.

InputAndMenus/game.lua
```lua
-- Add a new enemy every 3 seconds
nextEnemy = nextEnemy - 1

if nextEnemy < 0 then
    -- 3 seconds have passed, so create a new ship
    local newShip = Spaceship( )
    ships[ #ships + 1 ] = newShip

    -- Add a touch event listener to the ship
    newShip.spriteInstance:addEventListener( "touch", tappedShip )

    -- Reset the enemy counter
    nextEnemy = 90

end
```

This code will call a function called tappedShip(), so our next step is to write it. We want this function to mark the ships as inactive, so we'll set the self.isAlive variable to false.

It's also a good idea to check the touch event's phase before processing the loop, since the player may have started tapping or finished tapping. In this case, toggle the ship's isAlive variable only if the player has started tapping. This means we'll look for the 'began' value, which is triggered when the player taps the screen. Corona also triggers touch events when the users move their fingers ('moved'), when they lift them ('ended'), or when the system cancels tracking the touch ('cancelled'). We can use those for tapping and dragging in games, but we don't need to know how to use them yet.

InputAndMenus/game.lua
```lua
-- Function triggered when a spaceship is tapped
local tappedShip = function( event )
    -- Mark the ship as dead
    event.target.object.isAlive = false
end
```

Now that you've coded the tappedShip() function, there won't be any visible changes in the game; we're changing the value of a variable, and we're not doing anything else with it. The main change is that the ships are marked for deletion, so we'll have an easier time when updating the game loop to remove them.

Updating Spaceships

When we updated spaceships in the previous chapter, we focused on moving them in the tick() function. The program loops through the list of ships and calls their update() function, which updates the ship coordinates. If the ship has reached the planet, then it stops moving. Instead of doing this, we can remove the ship completely so that it stops consuming resources. We can use those resources to add more ships to continue the invasion.

In the previous chapter, we placed a check that moved the ships only whenever the hypotenuse to the center of the planet was greater than 20 (in other words, its square was greater than 400). Now, update the code to always move the ships, and remove the ships whenever they go past that area.

In the update() function code, place the movement code outside the distance check, and mark the unit as inactive if the distance is less than 20 by setting its isAlive variable to false.

InputAndMenus/spaceship.lua
```lua
-- Move the sprite
self:move( self.speed * dx / hyp, self.speed * dy / hyp )
-- Check the ship is not too close to the planet
if hyp < PLANET_RADIUS then
    self.isAlive = false
end
```

Now build a function called toggleDelete() for the ships. Whenever we call that function, it will return true if the ship has to be deleted. The function itself has to check the variable isAlive in the ship. If the ship is not alive, delete it by calling removeSelf().

InputAndMenus/spaceship.lua
```lua
function Spaceship:toggleDelete( )
    -- The ship must be deleted if it's marked as dead
    if( self.isAlive == false ) then
        return true
    end
    -- The ship is alive
    return false
end
```

The last step is to use the toggleDelete() function in the game loop. To do this, check whether toggleDelete() returns true, which means that the ship has to be removed. Here's where looping backward (from #ships to 1) is really helpful because we can delete elements from the ships table without having to change the loop variable.

To remove the ship from the table, call removeMe(), which we already wrote in the previous chapter. There's also an auxiliary function that will come in handy, called removeTableRows(), in auxiliary.lua in the book's chapter files. If you don't want to write your own table-manipulation functions, you can use this one to delete an element from an array.

InputAndMenus/game.lua
```lua
-- This function will update our enemies each frame
function updateEnemies( )
    -- Loop through each of the enemies and update them
    for i = #ships, 1, -1 do
        ships[ i ]:update( )
        -- Remove dead ships
        if ( ships[ i ]:toggleDelete( ) == true ) then
            ships[ i ]:removeMe( )
            removeTableRows( ships, i )
        end
    end
end
```

This is a good time to check the console for possible errors. Try to compile the game now and wait for the ships to get to the planet. Corona has a verbose console that tells us whenever there are bugs or incorrect variables. If something isn't working properly, we'll usually get detailed error logs to help us track the problem. These error logs may not be as helpful as those you'd get when using traditional programming languages, but they're much more helpful than error messages from development tools such as Flash.

4.3 Displaying Scenes Using the Storyboard API

One of the best features of the Corona SDK is its Storyboard application programming interface (API). So far, we have used only one scene for our main game, but we can use multiple scenes to handle different parts of the game. From now on, we'll have several files that come from the scenetemplate.lua template. Code related to each scene will go into that scene file so that it's easier to find it whenever you want to change something.

We will usually divide a game into scenes that are not related to each other, just like we would do with a film, so that we can work on them independently. We can use a scene for the menu and another one for the game. For more complicated games, you can add scenes for high-score screens, game-over stages, in-game shops, or even splash screens to promote your game studio.

Whenever you tell Corona to change scenes, in-game objects within the scene image group will be removed automatically. This makes it really easy to change from the game to the main menu without having to remove in-game elements manually.

It's easy to work with scenes in Corona. You have to add objects to the stage whenever the players enter a scene, and make sure that you remove all those objects as soon as the players exit the scene.

The Corona simulator comes with a storyboard template, which creates a new document with four placeholder functions: createScene(), enterScene(), exitScene(), and destroyScene(). The names of these functions are quite self-explanatory, but let's take a look at what they do.

- createScene() is called when the scene is first created. This comes before the player sees anything, so it's good to add the initial graphics here.

- enterScene() is called as soon as the scene is completely displayed. If you have any scene-transition effects in place, then those go before the enterScene() function. If you plan to make a long scene transition, add tapping interactions in this function to avoid accidental taps during the scene transition.

- exitScene() is called just before going out of the scene (to another scene). If you don't want players to do anything during a scene transition, this is the function you'll want to modify. Remove interactivity and any other possible source of unwanted actions here.

- destroyScene() is the last function called when the program exits the scene. This function is called once the player can't see anything in the scene. Use it to remove graphics and visual elements to clean up unused memory resources.

Corona won't load any of the scenes unless it's instructed to do so. When a project is run, Corona processes the main.lua file. When we create a new storyboard project, Corona makes this file automatically and loads scenetemplate.lua. In the previous chapter, we updated it to go to the game.lua scene. If we want to display the menu instead, we have to change only that line.

Adding a Main Menu

Let's keep our game simple and add only a basic menu scene to the game. We'll draw an image on the background, and we'll move to the game whenever the user taps the stage.

Start by making a new scene document using Corona's template-creation feature and change the filename to something self-explanatory, such as menu.lua. Update the main game file, main.lua, so that it loads the new scene you created. Use display.setStatusBar() to hide the status bar; we don't want to see it in most games.

InputAndMenus/main.lua

```
-- hide the status bar
display.setStatusBar(display.HiddenStatusBar)
-- Require the storyboard API and go to the menu scene
local storyboard = require "storyboard"
storyboard.gotoScene( "menu" )
```

You can load an image using the display.newImage() function. Pass the image name as a parameter, and Corona does the rest of the work. It's important to insert() the image onto the scene group after loading it, because otherwise it'll be on top of all the onscreen elements. As well as that, it'll be much easier to remove objects in scene transitions if they're in their corresponding scene groups.

Now load and insert an image called menu_bg.jpg, which you can find in this chapter's code files.

InputAndMenus/menu.lua

```
-- Add an image to the scene
local bgimage = display.newImage("images/menu_bg.jpg")
group:insert( bgimage )
```

The image looks nice (Figure 18, *The game's main menu*, on page 61), but it doesn't let us play the game anymore, so we have to add interactivity to it.

Corona has a great listener for touch-based events, called touch. Add an event listener to the image using addEventListener(), and pass touch and a function that has to be called whenever the scene is tapped. We can call the function gotoGame().

Figure 18—The game's main menu

InputAndMenus/menu.lua
```
bgimage:addEventListener( "touch", gotoGame )
```

As you probably guessed, we now have to write the contents of gotoGame(). Since we're calling the function using an event listener, it will receive an event as a parameter. Let's be redundant and call the event event. Now, since tap states can be pressing, moving, or lifting the finger from the screen, the function has to listen to only one of the events. Make the function check that the event phase property is equal to "began" (or "ended", if you prefer) and trigger a scene transition. In Corona, we trigger storyboard transitions using the same call that comes with the premade template: storyboard.gotoScene().

InputAndMenus/menu.lua
```
-- Touch event listener for the menu's background image
-- Goes to the game scene
local gotoGame = function( event )
    -- Only process the event if the player started the tap
    if event.phase == "ended" then
        storyboard.gotoScene( "game" )
    end
end
```

That's it! Scene transitions are that easy. Corona does most of the work for us, and we only have to make sure that we write the scene names properly.

If you're afraid of misspelling scene names, feel free to use a text variable with the different names. That way, if a scene transition works once, then the name is written properly and you don't have to test all the other appearances.

4.4 Adding Buttons

Even though it's great to add custom tap-based input to interact with units in our games, it's always good to have reusable code for stuff we use frequently, such as buttons. Unless you're making a really simple game, you'll need buttons for the main menu, some of the interfaces, and even online-sharing functions. You can code them from scratch each time you need them, but it's much faster and safer to code them once and reuse them. That way you're sure that the button code works, saving you hours of testing.

When we think of buttons, we think of hit areas, button images, interactivity, and even a pressed state. We need a hit area because we want the user to hit the button easily, even if the button has strange fonts or invisible images. Images are needed in a game because it wouldn't look nice to have text-based buttons, and we need interactivity because a button has to do something to be a button instead of an image.

Corona comes with predefined functions in its Widget API that let us build buttons really quickly. Start by loading the widget class, which lets us build new buttons.

InputAndMenus/menu.lua
```
-- Require the widget class
widget = require "widget"
```

After adding the widget class, you can build a button using a method called widget.newButton(). This function receives several parameters as a Lua table: an id, the button's left and top coordinates, the label text to be displayed, the width and height, and the cornerRadius if you want rounded corners. You also need to pass the onEvent() function you want to get called whenever the user clicks the button.

Build a new Play button in the game's main menu using the widget.newButton() function. Make it a reasonable size, such as 100×30, and place it near the bottom of the screen. Make it call the gotoGame() function we wrote earlier.

InputAndMenus/menu.lua
```
-- Build a "Play" button
local playButton = widget.newButton{
    id = "btnplay",
    label = "Play",
    left = 100,
    top = 200,
    width = 120,
```

```
    height = 40,
    cornerRadius = 10,
    onEvent = gotoGame
}
group:insert( playButton )
```

I can almost hear you saying, "But that's a really ugly button!" I agree; a black-and-white button can be fine for serious apps, but it doesn't look very good in games.

We can use Corona's sprite sheet system to pass a sprite sheet where we want to get the images from. The button's default state will show the frame number passed as a variable called defaultFrame, and the pressed state will change this frame to the frame number we passed in overFrame (as shown in the image here).

Using these new variables, update the button so that it uses the user-interface (UI) sprite sheet called menuSheets, and frame number 1 as the default state and 2 as the pressed state (see Figure 20, *Play button*).

InputAndMenus/menu.lua
```
-- Create a new sprite sheet
menuSheets = graphics.newImageSheet( "images/menu_buttons.png",
    { width = 120, height = 40, numFrames = 2 } )

local playButton = widget.newButton{
    -- Make the button use the sprite sheet
    sheet = menuSheets,
    defaultFrame = 1,
    overFrame = 2,
}
```

That's it! Using an image instead of the default button design was that simple. Don't you love Corona already? At this point, you can also remove the links on the main menu's background image. Since we've already coded an alternative button, there's no need to include two ways to start the game.

4.5 Adding Lives and Difficulty

Right now, the game has lots of enemies, but it will keep going forever. It's important to limit the game so that it can end within a reasonable timeframe.

We can add a time limit for the level, make it really difficult, or add a progressive difficulty system. A time

Figure 20—Play button

limit can be frustrating for good players, because they might like the thrill of playing longer sessions. Increasing the difficulty will make the game too easy for some but too difficult for others, so it's not the ideal choice either.

That leaves us with the option to make the game easier at the beginning and make it harder as time advances. Let's do that and give players a few lives so that a small mistake doesn't kick them out of the game.

Limiting Lives

Limiting the number of lives a player has is really easy. We only need to keep track of a variable, such as lives, and update it each time that the player gains or loses one. In Planet Defender, we'll subtract a life each time an invading ship reaches the central planet, and we won't be adding any lives. The game will end when the player loses all lives.

Let's start by creating the lives variable. Set it to 3, which seems like a reasonable number; players can make a few mistakes, but they won't be forced to play forever.

InputAndMenus/game.lua
```
-- Start tracking player lives
lives = 3
```

When the game removes a ship that has moved too close to the planet, it means the player didn't destroy it in time. Update the code so that it subtracts a life after removing the spaceship.

Since the game counts the number of remaining lives, it makes sense to check whether the player has run out of lives. If the number of lives left is equal to zero, the game has ended, so call the Storyboard API again to change scenes. If there are no lives left, the game sends players to a game-over scene using storyboard.gotoScene(). (See Figure 21, *Game-over scene*, on page 65.)

InputAndMenus/game.lua
```
for i = #ships, 1, -1 do
    -- Remove dead ships
    if ( ships[ i ]:toggleDelete( ) == true ) then
        -- If the ship was not killed by the player, subtract a life
        if ( ships[ i ].wasKilled == false ) then
            lives = lives - 1
        end
    end
end
-- Check the number of lives
if lives <= 0 then
    storyboard.gotoScene( "gameover" )
end
```

Figure 21—Game-over scene

Before compiling the app, create a new storyboard scene (using the default Corona template) for the game-over screen. We don't really want to get into too much work here, so just add an image that says "game over" to the scene-creation function. Add an event listener to return to the menu (using addEventListener() and storyboard:gotoScene()), but do so with a small delay. That way, if players tap the screen a millisecond late, they won't accidentally return to the menu.

InputAndMenus/gameover.lua

```
-- Menu listener function. Add a touch listener to the image
function addMenuListener( event )
    bgimage:addEventListener( "touch", gotoMenu )
end


-- Add an image during the scene creation process
function scene:createScene( event )
    local group = self.view

    -- Add a background image to the game over scene
    bgimage = display.newImage( "images/game_over.jpg" )
    group:insert( bgimage )

end
```

It's great to have a lives system in a game, but players will need to know how many lives they have left. Otherwise, losing the game will just feel random. We'll display their lives using a small image in a group.

In the image sheets in this chapter, the life icon is called heart. Add it three times, updating the x-coordinate with each life so that the images don't all appear in the same location.

InputAndMenus/game.lua
```
-- Display the lives
for i = 1, 3 do
    local lifeSprite = display.newImage( imageSheet,
        spritedata:getFrameIndex( IMG_LIFE ) )
    lifeSprite.x = 15 * i - 5
    lifeSprite.y = 10
    lifeGroup:insert( lifeSprite )
end
```

Since we've just created a set of display objects, we have to remove one each time a life is lost. In this case, we remove the topmost object because it's the rightmost life icon. If you've decided to paint the lives in a different order, just make sure to delete one that makes sense. A UI layout can stop "feeling right" if icons aren't spread out evenly.

Add the call to remove() to the code after you subtract a life from the player.

InputAndMenus/game.lua
```
lifeGroup[ lifeGroup.numChildren ]:removeSelf( )
```

Figure 23—Player lives

Try to compile the app to check that lives are shown properly and that they're subtracted. Right now, the game will look much more complete (as shown in the figure here).

Also test whether the game-over screen appears properly—it's easy to make a simple mistake in a scene change, and it's better to spot it before the players do!

Making It More Challenging

Enemies are being added periodically so far, but that's because of the constant difficulty level in the game. We can change difficulty in many ways, but a very easy solution is to increase the number of enemies gradually. That way, inexperienced players will be able to play for a while, and experienced players will have lots of fun when the game becomes too fast even for them.

We can use a logarithmic equation to increase the speed at which we add our ships. To do this, use a shipsAdded variable to store the number of ships we've added to the game.

InputAndMenus/game.lua
```
-- Create a variable to store the number of ships added
shipsAdded = 0
```

Each time the game adds a ship, add 1 to the variable. Then, update nextEnemy so the next ship can appear after 2000 / (math.log(shipsAdded / 5) + 1) milliseconds. Why logarithmic? That means ships will be added faster each time—but up to a certain limit to avoid making the game ridiculously difficult.

Since Corona works based on frames and a game's frame rate is usually 60 frames per second, there isn't much point in being too accurate when calculating the time required to add the next ship. If you want, update the nextEnemy variable to round it down.

InputAndMenus/game.lua
```
-- Reset the enemy counter
shipsAdded = shipsAdded + 1
nextEnemy = 33 / ( math.log( 1 + shipsAdded / 5 ) + 1 )
```

Voilà! Our game has an incremental difficulty system. It's great for new players because it lets them play for several seconds, but it's also great for veterans because ships will be added faster each time. Since we're using logarithms, the speed will increase quickly at the beginning and slowly later. That way, the speed will never increase abruptly, and we won't receive complaints from frustrated players.

4.6 Exercises and Expansion Options

Now that we have finished the chapter, here are some ideas you can try to improve this game.

Power-Ups

In this app, we only add enemies to our game, and the goal is to stop them from reaching our planet. We can add power-ups using the same system as we've used with the ships. Add them randomly after a certain amount of time, and update them in each frame. If players tap them, they can get an extra life. If they don't tap them, then the program needs to remove them eventually. You can do this by adding a frame counter and deleting the power-up if it's inactive after 90 frames (3 seconds) or so.

Splash Screen

Have you noticed splash screens at the start of many games? Developers show their logo for a few seconds before getting into the action. The Storyboard API makes this really easy, because you can use a new scene to show the logo. In the storyboard.gotoScene() function, you can pass "fade", 800 as the second (effect name) and third (transition time) parameters to make the scene fade instead of showing an abrupt transition. Most games show a splash screen using fade, but you can also play with SlideDown, fromRight, or any other transition-effect name.

Credits Screen

It's sometimes great to add a credits page to your game just in case somebody wants to check who developed it (and maybe download some of your other games). Since you've learned about scene transitions, it's easy to make a new scene that shows your logo, with a button to go back. Make sure you add your studio name or any games you want to mention there.

4.7   What We Covered

At this point, we know how to use most forms of input for our games. We can now make our units and objects interactive to make apps react to players' actions. Corona also lets us add buttons to make our games easier to use and more intuitive for players, and the Storyboard API is great to make scene transitions in our games without having to code everything manually.

From now on, we'll reuse these tools to make more-complex games. The next app we'll make is a vertical-scrolling shooter, where we'll use everything we've learned from this app and add loading and saving tools, parallax, and explosions.

Part III

Vertical-Scrolling Shooter

Even though we successfully coded a little app in the previous part, we have to remember that games are about having fun. Our previous game was fun to play for a while, but really simple games can get old fairly quickly. In Part III we start experimenting with new gameplay mechanics that will help us write more engaging and enjoyable games.

CHAPTER 5

Representing Movement and Perspective

Now that we've covered how to use some of the basic Corona APIs and tools, it's time for us to move on to something more interesting. In this chapter, we'll start working on an entirely new scrolling and shooting game. It's OK, though; we'll still be playing with spaceships.

5.1 What You'll Learn

In this chapter we're going to sprint through most of the concepts we've already learned, but apply them in new ways to our new project. We'll do the following:

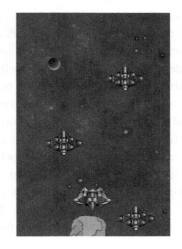

- Create a game with a player ship and several enemies
- Add movement and basic user input
- Move backgrounds at different speeds to give the impression of depth
- Generate asteroids randomly and move them down the screen

By the end of the chapter, we'll have created the basic framework for a classic scroller, and our app will look like the image shown earlier.

Before getting started with our new game, you should be comfortable with how to use classes, menus, added units, and movement, which we covered in Part II, *Planet Defender*, on page 15. Don't fret if you still find some of these steps challenging; you're still fairly new to Corona, and these steps can include tricky techniques.

5.2 Designing a Basic Scroller

Since we're creating a space shooter over the next few chapters, we'll call our new game Galactic Warfare. Before we can begin coding, we need to decide which features we want to include in the game. This will reduce the danger of feature creep and help us to know how to approach the problems we face as we work.

We'll have all of the following features in Galactic Warfare:

- A title screen
- Scrolling backgrounds
- Movement
- Shooting (both the player and enemies)
- Power-ups
- Collision detection
- Sound effects
- Background music

To add all these features, we'll have to learn how to use the Corona Sound API on page 107 and some functions of the Physics API on page 94. We'll also review layers and depth sorting in Corona and develop tricks for working with groups of sprites on the screen. Since this list represents a lot of new concepts, we'll spread them out over the next three chapters rather than jamming them all into one. In this chapter, we'll focus on coding the basic game framework. We'll add shooting and power-ups in Chapter 6, *Adding Shooting, Collisions, and Power-Ups*, on page 89. The last chapter in Part III, Chapter 7, *Adding Sound*, on page 107, will cover sound effects and background music.

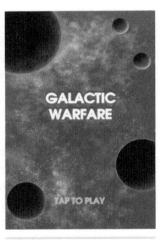

Figure 25—The Galactic Warfare title screen

5.3 Adding Menus and the Basic Framework

Before we can add code, we need to create an entirely new Corona project, so create a new project now or copy the storyboard templates from the Planet Defender game.

Copy menu.lua from your Planet Defender game folder, or copy it from the InputAndMenus folder in the book's code files and paste it into the Galactic Warfare folder. If you look at this chapter's source files, you'll see that the only change to make is the background image in the project folder (see Figure 25, *The Galactic Warfare title screen*, on page 72).

Also create a file called globals.lua. It will include the game's stage size, and we'll add the animation and sprite names we'll use as we code the game. We'll add many more image names to account for enemy graphics by the time we've developed the final version of the game, but for now let's store a few initial variables to support our work in this chapter.

Parallax/globals.lua
```
-- Stage size
WIDTH = 320
HEIGHT = 480

-- Player images
PLAYER_LEFT = "player_l"
PLAYER_CENTRE = "player"
PLAYER_RIGHT = "player_r"

-- Enemy images
ENEMY_1 = "enemy1"
ENEMY_2 = "enemy2"
ENEMY_3 = "enemy3"
```

After players lose all their lives, we'll have to display another storyboard scene to stop gameplay from continuing and to indicate to players that they've lost. To keep it simple, we can use storyboard.gotoScene() to make the game go back to the title screen instead of creating a new scene. However, to avoid wasting time debugging, let's wait until we reach Section 6.6, *Ending the Game*, on page 105, to add this feature. Adding losing conditions at the start of a game project would be annoying because we'd have to repeatedly start new games while debugging.

5.4 Adding and Removing Units

Before adding parallax effects, we'll implement the basic gameplay for Galactic Warfare. First, we need to add the player and all the enemies to the stage. This is similar to what we did in our Planet Defender game, but this time we'll add a static player and have the enemies move downward. Instead of tapping enemies to destroy them, we'll add bullets and let the player shoot at them to gain bonuses like extra lives.

Start by creating an empty storyboard scene called game.lua. You can copy the default scene template generated when you created the project, or you can use the one in the chapter's code files.

For this game, we'll use classes to store ship sprites and data like we did for the Planet Defender game. That way, we'll be able to work with enemies more comfortably. Remember how we used the Class.lua file? We'll reuse it without making any changes, so we can copy it directly into our project's folder.

Building a Unit Class

Let's begin by creating a Unit class that will be in charge of storing our ship sprites, their speed and location, and the images they should display. To make player ship movement more`realistic, we'll display a different image whenever the player's ship steers, but since both player and enemy ships will inherit from this class, we'll need to make it as flexible as possible. Let's start by taking a look at the ship sprite sheet, shown in the figure here.

This is the set of images we'll use to represent the ships. Like in the previous chapters, the images are a bit disorganized instead of regularly arranged because the sprite file has been created by a sprite-exporting program called TexturePacker. Since the file has been generated automatically, we can safely ignore its content. Doing this manually, as we discussed when we built Planet Defender, takes a lot more work. Just imagine having to write texture-definition tables for dozens or even hundreds of sprites!

The Unit constructor first has to create a new sprite using one of the ships in the sprite sheet. Then it has to add it to a display group with all the other units to easily remove the unit from the screen. The last step is to set its starting position and speed.

Parallax/unit.lua
```
Unit = Class( )
-- Unit constructor
function Unit:new( group, spriteSet )
    -- Create a new sprite and add it to the group
    -- local spriteInstance = sprite.newSprite( spriteSet )
    local spriteInstance = display.newSprite( imagesheet,
        spriteSequences.shipsSequence )

    spriteInstance:setReferencePoint( display.CenterReferencePoint )
    spriteInstance.x = -50
    spriteInstance.y = -50

    group:insert( spriteInstance )
    self.spriteInstance = spriteInstance
end
```

We also need functions to tell the units to move and to delete them whenever they are destroyed or exit the screen, so create the setPosition(), move(), toggleDelete(), and removeMe() functions. As was the case in Planet Defender, move() will move the unit each frame, toggleDelete() will return true if it is out of bounds, and removeMe() will remove the sprite. The setPosition() function will teleport the unit to any location we want.

```
Parallax/unit.lua
-- Set the unit's position
function Unit:setPosition( x, y )
    self.spriteInstance.x = x
    self.spriteInstance.y = y
    self.x = x
    self.y = y
end
-- Move the unit in the y direction
function Unit:move( )
    self.y = self.y + self.vy
    self.spriteInstance.rotation = 0
    self.spriteInstance.y = self.y
    self.spriteInstance.x = self.x
end
-- Check whether the unit is out of bounds
function Unit:toggleDelete( )
    if (( self.y < -20 ) or ( self.y > 500 )) then
        return true
    end
    return false
end
-- Remove the unit
function Unit:removeMe( )
    self.spriteInstance:removeSelf( )
    self.spriteInstance = nil
end
```

We're done with the basic unit framework. From now on, we'll be able to call these functions from the game to move and update the ships.

Adding the Player's Ship

The player's ship will use the Unit class, but we'll modify it to update movement with reference to a target position. Players will control their ships by touching the area of the screen that they want to move to. We'll update the default Unit:move() function in the Player class so that movement depends on user input rather than occurring at constant speeds.

The Unit constructor we wrote a moment ago will create the sprite and hide it off-screen. This function starts after that point, so center the ship horizontally and put it near the bottom so that players have time to avoid incoming enemies and obstacles. Also, change the default enemy ship sprite to match the player's ship sprite. It should be different so users don't visually confuse it with an enemy ship.

Parallax/unit.lua
```lua
Player = Class( Unit )

-- Player constructor
function Player:new( group, spriteSet )
    self.spriteInstance.x = WIDTH / 2
    self.spriteInstance.y = 400
    self.x = self.spriteInstance.x
    self.y = self.spriteInstance.y
    -- Don't set a target coordinate when the game starts
    self.targetX = self.spriteInstance.x
    self.targetY = self.spriteInstance.y
    -- Display the player's ship
    self.spriteInstance:setSequence( PLAYER_CENTRE )
end
```

This is a good time to make sure that the units and enemies can be added to the stage without causing Corona errors. Start by creating an imageSheet in the createScene() method and adding the ship sprites to the game using sprite.add(). After that, initialize the player's ship by calling the Player() constructor using Player(group, imageSheet).

Parallax/game.lua
```lua
-- Initialize the player
playerInstance = Player( group, spriteSet )
```

To move the player, write two functions: setTargetPosition() and resetTargetPosition(). We'll call setTargetPosition() whenever the player's ship moves somewhere, and call resetTargetPosition() to stop the ship's movement. (We'll flesh out the move() function in *Handling Player Input*, on page 78.)

Parallax/unit.lua
```lua
-- Set the player's target coordinates
function Player:setTargetPosition( x, y )
    self.targetX = x
    self.targetY = y
end
-- Remove target coordinates from the player's ship
function Player:resetTargetPosition( )
    self.targetX = self.spriteInstance.x
    self.targetY = self.spriteInstance.y
end
-- Move the player
function Player:move( )
end
```

Once we add interactivity to the game, these functions will store a target position for the player whenever users tap the screen. Whenever the user lifts the finger from the screen, the target position will be reset to the current position. We won't handle the interactions just yet, though.

Defining the Enemy Class

We want enemies to start at random locations on the screen and move downward. To do that, write the Enemy() constructor to set a random position for the sprite. Then set the enemy's vertical (y) speed so that enemies do, in fact, move downward.

```
Parallax/unit.lua
Enemy = Class( Unit )
-- Enemy constructor
function Enemy:new( group, spriteSet )
    -- Set position and speed
    self.x = 10 + math.random( 300 )
    self.y = -10
    self.vy = 3
    self.spriteInstance.x = self.x
    self.spriteInstance.y = self.y
    -- Prepare the enemy's sprite
    self.spriteInstance:setSequence( ENEMY_1 )
end
```

Remember how we used a constant enemy spawn rate that increased with time in Planet Defender? In Galactic Warfare, we'll add a bit of randomness. Each time the program adds an enemy, we'll reset a counter using Corona's random() function. Finally, we'll add a value to the randomly generated number to make sure that enemies are not appearing too quickly. Otherwise, an unlucky player might encounter a new enemy ship in each frame.

```
Parallax/game.lua
-- addEnemies
-- Adds an enemy if we've waited enough time
local function addEnemies( group )
    lastEnemy = lastEnemy - 1

    if ( lastEnemy <= 0 ) then

        -- Add the enemy
        lastEnemy = math.random( ENEMY_DELAY ) + ENEMY_DELAY
        enemies[ #enemies + 1 ] = Enemy( group, spriteSet )
    end

end
```

Each time a new enemy is added, the counter is reset to a random number between ENEMY_DELAY and twice that number. This makes the game less predictable. Ships will sometimes appear to come in waves or more sporadically.

Moving the Units on the Screen

Earlier we said that we want enemies to move downward at a constant speed, and we want the player's ship to spin right or left depending on its horizontal speed. Let's add functions to implement these behaviors now.

Making the Enemies Move

As was the case with Planet Defender, we'll work with a changing number of enemies onscreen, which means using dynamic arrays again. Since we plan to remove enemies as they get killed, we'll loop backward through the table to avoid skipping elements as it shrinks.

The first thing we need to do to update the enemies in each frame is to loop from the total number of enemies to 1. For each enemy, begin by calling its move() function to update its position and then delete it if it goes out of bounds. To do this, use the toggleDelete() and removeMe() functions we defined in *Defining the Enemy Class*, on page 77. In this type of loop, remember that Corona uses table indices from 1 to n, instead of 0 to (n - 1) like many other languages.

Parallax/game.lua
```
-- Update the enemies
local function updateEnemies( group )
    -- Loop through all the enemies
    --  (backwards in case we remove some from the table)
    for i = #enemies, 1, -1 do
        -- Move the enemy
        enemies[ i ]:move( )
        -- Delete inactive enemies
        if ( enemies[ i ]:toggleDelete( ) == true ) then
            -- Remove the enemy
            enemies[ i ]:removeMe( )
            removeTableRows( enemies, i, 1 )
        end
    end
end
```

If you compile the game, you'll be able to see the enemies move, but the player doesn't move yet. Let's update the player's ship to make the game more fun.

Handling Player Input

Remember how we checked for input in the Planet Defender game? We'll do the same thing here. First add an event listener to the scene by calling addEventListener(). That way, as soon as a player touches the screen, the program will trigger the event function. As long as the player keeps touching, our function will continue to update the ship's target location. We'll stop the ship's movement when the player stops pressing the screen.

Parallax/game.lua

```lua
-- Handles the game's touch event listener and
--     updates the player's position accordingly
local function onPlayerTouch( event )
    if event.phase ~= "ended" then
        -- If the player keeps pressing the screen,
        --     save the touch location as the target position
        playerInstance:setTargetPosition( event.x, event.y )
    else
        -- When the touch event ends, stop moving the player
        playerInstance:resetTargetPosition( )
    end
end
```

To make movement a bit more fun for the player, we can make the ship's movement behave like a spring—we'll move the player's ship toward the touch location more quickly when the ship is farther away from it. We can use speed = constant * distanceToTouch to calculate the speed at which our spaceship should move. We can see this in the following figure.

Player ship movement needs to be coded differently from enemy ship movement because it depends on player input. We'll replace the move() function in the Unit class and write something else for player movement. The class structure we use allows us to overwrite functions—it will always look for methods in the class we're using before looking for an equivalent method in the base class. This means we can define a Player:move() method, and the program will run it instead of the Unit:move() method when we're moving our player. (The use of two different methods in this way is called *overloading*.)

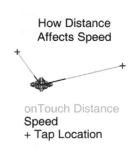

How Distance
Affects Speed

onTouch Distance
Speed
+ Tap Location

Figure 27—Calculating the player's movement

In the Player:move() function, start by using the self.target.x target position variable we defined earlier. Calculate the difference between that and the ship's current position (self.x), and use that to calculate the speed. If the player has to move right or left, swap the animation image using the sprite prepare() and play() functions for the PLAYER_RIGHT and PLAYER_LEFT animations that we stored in the globals.lua file.

Parallax/unit.lua
```lua
-- Move the player
function Player:move( )
    -- Calculate the distance to the target
    local dx = self.targetX - self.x
    local dy = self.targetY - self.y
    dx = dx / PLAYER_SPEED_COEFF
    local vx = math.max( math.min( PLAYER_MAXSPEED, dx ), -PLAYER_MAXSPEED )
    self.x = self.x + vx
    self.spriteInstance.x = self.x

    -- Steer the ship right or left if it's moving horizontally
    if ( self.targetX > self.spriteInstance.x + 15 ) then
        self.spriteInstance:setSequence( PLAYER_RIGHT )
    elseif ( self.targetX < self.spriteInstance.x - 15 ) then
        self.spriteInstance:setSequence( PLAYER_LEFT )
    else
        self.spriteInstance:setSequence( PLAYER_CENTRE )
    end
end
```

Try to compile the program now to see the ship in action. If you tap the screen, the ship will move to your finger's x-coordinate and ignore its y position.

5.5 Displaying Scrolling Backgrounds and Parallax Effects

Though it's nice to see enemies move around the screen, the static background doesn't look completely right because in most games players see the background move. To represent movement, we could design a complex 3D scene and render it, but for 2D games we can take the easy path and use a scrolling image.

The figure here shows one of the main ways of displaying scrolling backgrounds. We use two identical images (that can be tiled) and move them until the first one is no longer visible. Once this is the case, we move them back to their starting position and repeat the loop.

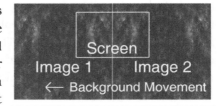

Figure 28—Scrolling backgrounds

Adapting to Relative Movement

In our Planet Defender game we had a fixed camera (a static view of the game world), and the spaceships moved around the visible area. In Galactic Warfare we'll focus our camera on the player's spaceship. When the player moves horizontally, the camera will remain still, but when the player moves vertically, we'll follow the ship through the game world.

Moving the camera changes the way that objects in the game need to move. As the camera moves, objects will need to move more quickly or more slowly (across more or fewer pixels) relative to the player's ship. You can see this in the following figure.

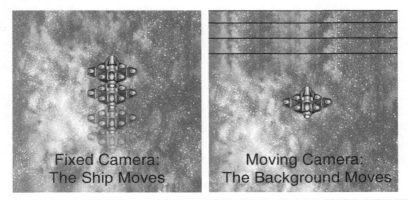

Figure 29—Camera types

Our ship will move back and forth across the screen in the horizontal direction, but we'll follow the player's vertical movements and adjust enemy speeds accordingly. To take this into account and provide realistic movement, we have to recalculate vertical object velocities using this formula:

velocity = absoluteVelocity - cameraVelocity

This is equivalent to saying that we move objects by adding both their speed and the player's speed in pixels to their y-coordinates.

Increasing Realism Using a Parallax Effect

We could just add object speeds to their coordinates with each tick and the objects in the foreground would move realistically. However, if you look at distant objects from a moving car, you'll agree that they don't seem to move at the same speed as nearby objects. To represent this in games, we can use an effect called *parallax* that moves background layers more slowly than foreground layers. Let's see how it works by looking at two still images from the same scene, as shown in Figure 30, *Parallax movement*, on page 82.

An easy way to represent the effect we see when we move the camera is to simulate movement for objects using the equation mentioned earlier and to move backgrounds less than the objects in front of them. To create this effect, we'll multiply background speeds by a number less than the player's speed. We'll usually test several values until one of them looks right with the speed

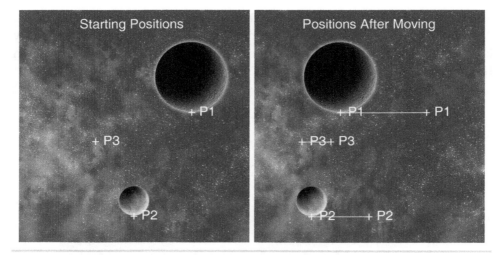

Figure 30—Parallax movement

of movement—there's no need to calculate background speeds using math. As long as parallax background speeds are slower than foreground speeds, the effect will be more or less realistic. If backgrounds move too quickly, it'll be confusing because ships will appear to move backward.

Using the previous equation, our space backgrounds will move more slowly and give the impression of being farther away. Each parallax layer has a coefficient that decreases its movement speed; setting these coefficients carefully will allow us to give the impression of distance or depth in our background. Let's start by defining the variables we'll use to store the two parallax groups called parallax1 and parallax2.

Parallax/game.lua
```
local parallax1, parallax2
```

Now write a function to load an image and display it twice in the background. Store the images in a group so that we can move them both at the same time afterward. That way, we'll be able to move each group down and reset its position as soon as the first image moves out of bounds.

Parallax/game.lua
```
-- Load a background image and add it to a parallax layer
function loadParallaxLayer( sceneGroup, imageName )
    -- Create a group
    local parallaxGroup = display.newGroup( )

    -- Load the background image twice and add them to the group
    local bgImage = display.newImage( imageName )
```

```
parallaxGroup:insert( bgImage )
bgImage:setReferencePoint( display.TopLeftReferencePoint )
bgImage.y = 0

bgImage = display.newImage( imageName )
parallaxGroup:insert( bgImage )
bgImage:setReferencePoint( display.TopLeftReferencePoint )
bgImage.y = bgImage.height

-- Add the parallax group to the scene
sceneGroup:insert( parallaxGroup )
parallaxGroup:setReferencePoint( display.CenterLeftReferencePoint )
parallaxGroup.y = 0

-- Return the group
return parallaxGroup
end
```

Now that we have our function, we'll call it twice from the game's scene:createScene() function in game.lua. We'll use two parallax layers in our game. Using only two layers will make it easy to code while still creating our desired effect.

Parallax/game.lua
```
-- Create the parallax layers
parallax2 = loadParallaxLayer( group, "images/parallaxbg.jpg" )
parallax1 = loadParallaxLayer( group, "images/parallaxfg.png" )
```

In the scene:enterScene() function, we'll have to update the scene group's position so that it is at (0, 0). Otherwise, as we're using large images, the group will appear in the center of the stage.

Parallax/game.lua
```
group.yReference = 0
group.y = 0
```

If we compile the program now, the two background layers will be positioned statically relative to one another. It looks pretty, but it won't be parallax (the impression of depth) until we add relative movement, so let's set speed coefficients for each layer to make the foreground layer appear to move more quickly. Define two variables, parallaxCoefficient1 and parallaxCoefficient2, with values of 2 and 1, respectively.

Parallax/globals.lua
```
-- Parallax layer speeds
parallaxCoefficient1 = 2
parallaxCoefficient2 = 1
```

Now that we've chosen two straightforward coefficients, create a new function that will be called from the game's tick() function. The new function adds the parallax speed coefficients when updating each layer. With each tick, check whether the first image in each group has gone out of bounds, and move the group up by half its height if it has so that the background scrolling is seamless. Remember that each image is repeated in the group, so moving the object by one image's height just shows the other one.

Parallax/game.lua
```lua
-- Updates the parallax each frame
local function updateParallax( )
    -- Move in the y direction (using the coefficient in globals.lua)
    parallax2.y = parallax2.y + parallaxCoefficient2
    parallax1.y = parallax1.y + parallaxCoefficient1

    -- Reset the layers' positions if they scroll out of the scene
    if parallax2.y >= parallax2[1].height then
        parallax2.y = parallax2.y - parallax2[1].height
    end
    if parallax1.y >= parallax1[1].height then
        parallax1.y = parallax1.y - parallax1[1].height
    end
end
```

Now we'll add a call to our newly created function from the game tick() function, and our parallax implementation will be done.

Parallax/game.lua
```lua
-- Update the parallax layers
updateParallax( )
```

5.6 Generating Random Backgrounds

Moving the ship and shooting at enemies might be too easy to keep some players interested, so we'll make their lives a bit harder in order to keep them focused and entertained. What if we add a few asteroids to make backgrounds more varied? To do this, we'll add a new layer behind enemy ships and place the asteroids there. That way, they won't obscure enemies or other foreground layers from the game.

Creating Random Asteroids

Let's start by coding an algorithm that creates random asteroids, rotates them, and adds a few craters to make them unique.

We'll use one of the large asteroid images in the chapter folder as the starting point for our asteroids. To add some variation to the image, we'll add a crater at a random location. We could easily expand this code to add a different number of craters or even add space dust or other effects. Making random asteroids is like making pizza—you add ingredients depending on your tastes.

Let's define a few constants to store information about our asteroids. We have three asteroid images and four craters at specific locations in our ship sprites table, so store those details in variables. Also define a variable to store the animation names we'll use. In this project, we have asteroid background image names that start with asteroid_ and are followed by a number from 1 to 3, and we have crater images that start with crater_, followed by a number from 1 to 4. Whenever we want to show one of these images, we can combine the prefix with one of the trailing numbers.

Parallax/globals.lua

```
-- Asteroid properties
ASTEROID_NAME = "asteroid_"
-- ASTEROID_FRAME = 16
ASTEROID_VARIANCE = 3
CRATER_NAME = "crater_"
-- CRATER_FRAME = ASTEROID_FRAME + ASTEROID_VARIANCE
CRATER_VARIANCE = 4
```

Now add the sprite data to Corona's sprite class so that we can access it in the future. Add all the asteroids and craters in our list, a total of seven sprites. Loop through the asteroids to add them to avoid having to type them individually. Also create two asteroid instances for our game. Since we have not coded the asteroid-creation file, call a placeholder function named makeAsteroid().

Parallax/game.lua

```
-- Create a group to hold the asteroids
asteroids = display.newGroup()
-- Create two asteroids and add them to the scene group
for i = 1, 2 do
    makeAsteroid( asteroids )
end
group:insert( asteroids )
```

In makeAsteroid(), put the asteroid and its crater together in a group so that we can move them both at the same time. Create a new sprite for each part of the asteroid (in other words, the center and the crater), and set the crater's relative coordinates so that it lands near the center of the asteroid. Since the base asteroids are not too round, any position between (10, 10) and (40, 40) will look fine.

Parallax/game.lua

```
-- Create an asteroid using our random images
function makeAsteroid( group )
    -- Create a group to store the asteroid
    local newGroup = display.newGroup()

    -- Choose a random image for the asteroid base and its crater
    local rockName = ASTEROID_NAME..math.random( ASTEROID_VARIANCE )
```

```lua
    local rock = display.newImage( imagesheet,
        spritedata:getFrameIndex(rockName) )
    local craterName = CRATER_NAME..math.random( CRATER_VARIANCE )
    local crater = display.newImage( imagesheet,
        spritedata:getFrameIndex(craterName) )

    -- Insert the images and set a random position for the group
    newGroup:insert( rock )
    newGroup:insert( crater )
    newGroup.x = 40 + math.random( 240 )
    newGroup.y = math.random( 480 )

    -- Set a random position for the crater
    rock.x = 0
    rock.y = 0
    crater.x = 10 + math.random( 40 )
    crater.y = 10 + math.random( 40 )

    -- Add everything to the asteroids layer
    group:insert( newGroup )
end
```

After our randomly generated asteroids are ready and look like the image here, we can add them to the game.

Moving the Asteroids

To avoid being messy and adding the code to update the asteroids to the tick() function, we'll write an updateAsteroids() function. We'll call this function in each tick(), so this function has to loop through all the asteroids once and move them at the speed of the top parallax layer.

Asteroid
Random crater

Use this loop to check whether the asteroids have moved out of bounds and to reset their positions if they have. To make the game a bit more varied, change their y position slightly, and completely randomize their x position. That way, when an asteroid leaves the screen, it won't appear in the same x position it used to have. Making the y change a bit will also change the y distance between both asteroids so that they're not separated by a constant distance.

Parallax/game.lua
```lua
-- updateAsteroids( )
-- Updates the asteroids' positions
function updateAsteroids( )
    for i = asteroids.numChildren, 1, -1 do
        -- Move the asteroid
        asteroids[ i ].y = asteroids[ i ].y + parallaxCoefficient1
```

```
        -- Move asteroids back to the top of the screen
        --    after they move out of bounds
        if asteroids[ i ].y > 530 then
            asteroids[ i ].y = -50 - math.random( 50 )
            asteroids[ i ].x = 40 + math.random( 240 )
        end
    end
end
```

We'll add a call to our newly defined updateAsteroids() function from the game tick() function so that the asteroids are updated each frame.

Parallax/game.lua
```
-- Update the asteroids
updateAsteroids( )
```

Try to compile the game now, and you'll see the random asteroids appear on the screen and move down, as shown in the figure here.

The asteroids in the background will move down as the game progresses, and the ships and background are still there. If you're feeling adventurous, add a physics body to the asteroid base and check for collisions with the player's ship. That would add an extra challenge to the game.

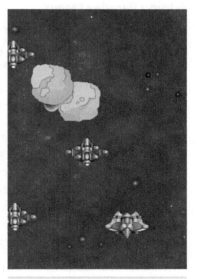

Figure 32—Galactic Warfare

5.7 Exercises and Expansion Options

Now that we've finished the chapter, here are some ideas you can try to improve this game.

Adding Enemy Formations

Random enemies are great to start with, but polished games sometimes spawn harder opponents. Update the enemy-spawning code so that we have a 5 percent chance of spawning seven spaceships in a V-formation, as shown in Figure 33, *Seven ships in a V-formation*, on page 88.

Displaying Vertical Movement

The player's ship moves only horizontally because we wanted to keep the camera's y position fixed. However, we might want to give players the option to travel faster (and maybe give them more points for it). Try to add one or two extra backgrounds to our game to make this possible. Hint: To add a

Figure 33—Seven ships in a V-formation

large number of backgrounds, we could store them in a group and change the updateParallax() method in game.lua to loop through all the parallax layers in the group instead of repeating the code.

Adding Parallax Layers

In this game, we added only two background layers with different parallax speeds. Can you change the game's code so that our app uses five parallax layers? Hint: One way to solve the problem is to define a Parallax class and use an instance for each layer.

5.8 What We Covered

Our goals for this chapter were to reuse earlier code to implement the basics of a vertical-scrolling game and to learn how to implement parallax and moving-camera effects. In the process, we built the first iteration of Galactic Warfare, which has moving enemy ships and an interactive player ship. We used groups to sort in-game objects into layers and used basic movement equations to create a parallax effect. Our ships all inherit from the Unit class, and we now know how to overload a function in Lua.

Our game will be easy to improve because we've divided the code into files that contain the major game-logic components. It might have been easier to code everything in the same file, but that would have made the code a lot more difficult to update in the future. With neater, better-structured code, we'll have an easier time in the next chapter as we add collisions and bullets and in Chapter 7, *Adding Sound*, on page 107, as we add sound to finish the game.

CHAPTER 6

Adding Shooting, Collisions, and Power-Ups

In Chapter 5, *Representing Movement and Perspective*, on page 71, we started a new game called Galactic Warfare. We laid the foundation for the game, creating a scrolling background with parallax layers while also implementing the basic mechanics of gameplay and movement. Galactic Warfare certainly has nice ships and backgrounds now, but people play games to take part in the action, not to watch nicely rendered scenery. It's time to get the player involved.

6.1 What You'll Learn

In this chapter, we'll do the following:

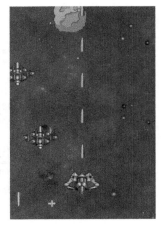

- Add the ability to fire missiles
- Implement animated explosion effects to represent damage
- Add power-ups to give bonuses to players
- Implement game-end conditions that players will struggle to avoid

Hang on tight, because we're about to add fun gameplay to Galactic Warfare! By the end of the chapter, our app will look like the image shown here.

6.2 Shooting

No space game is complete without shooting. We don't want Galactic Warfare to lack basic sci-fi features, so let's get right to business by adding shooting using the bullets shown in the following image.

As we did in the previous chapter, here we've used Tex-turePacker to combine the textures for our sprites; we've also used PhysicsEditor,[1] a program that automatically traces physics bodies from images, so we're ready to use our bullets immediately.

Just as we did with enemy ships, begin by defining a table for bullet sprites in the globals file. The table will link a name to each animation and will hold the location where we'll find the sprite definition in the shipsprites.lua file.

Shooting/globals.lua
```
-- Bullet variables
BULLET_RELOAD = 20
ENEMY_BULLET_RELOAD = 100

-- Bullet sprite
PLAYER_BULLET = "player_bullet"
ENEMY_BULLET = "enemy_bullet"
```

To make firing ships easy to implement, we'll build a Bullet class. We'll use it for bullets right now, but we'll focus on making it easy to expand so that we'll be able to reuse it in the future for power-ups and other kinds of projectiles.

Let's start the Bullet class by creating a constructor that stores a bullet's coordinates on the screen, its x and y speeds, and its status in the game (in play or already collided). Initialize the sprite depending on whether it's a friendly or enemy bullet (in other words, by checking the unit's type).

Shooting/bullet.lua
```
Bullet = Class( )
function Bullet:new( physics, group, spriteSet, unit )
    -- Create a new sprite, hide it out of bounds, and add it to the group
    local spriteInstance = display.newSprite( spriteSet,
        spriteSequences.bulletSequence )
    spriteInstance:setReferencePoint( display.CenterReferencePoint )
    spriteInstance.x = -50
    spriteInstance.y = -50
    group:insert( spriteInstance )
    self.spriteInstance = spriteInstance

    -- Mark the bullet as alive
    self.alive = true

    -- Prepare the bullet sprite
    self.spriteInstance.object = self
```

---

1. www.codeandweb.com/physicseditor

```
    local body, ydisplacement
    if unit.type == TYPE_PLAYER then
        -- Set starting speed and y difference from the shooting ship
        self.vy = -4
        ydisplacement = -10
        -- Assign the player sprite
        self.type = TYPE_PLAYER_BULLET
        self.spriteInstance:setSequence( PLAYER_BULLET )
    else
        -- Set starting speed and y difference from the shooting ship
        self.vy = 6 + parallaxCoefficient1
        ydisplacement = 10
        -- Set the enemy image
        self.type = TYPE_ENEMY_BULLET
        self.spriteInstance:setSequence( ENEMY_BULLET )
    end
    -- Set the starting coordinates
    spriteInstance.y = unit.y + ydisplacement
    spriteInstance.x = unit.x
    self.x = spriteInstance.x
    self.y = spriteInstance.y
end
```

To finish the Bullet class, write move(), toggleDelete(), and removeMe() functions. These functions parallel the ones we created for our units. move() updates the bullet, toggleDelete() checks to see whether the bullet should become inactive, and removeMe() removes any bullets that have been marked as inactive.

Shooting/bullet.lua
```
-- Move the unit in the y direction
function Bullet:move( )
    -- Update the y coordinate
    self.y = self.y + self.vy

    -- Reset coordinates
    self.spriteInstance.rotation = 0
    self.spriteInstance.y = self.y
    self.spriteInstance.x = self.x
end


-- Check whether the unit is out of bounds
function Bullet:toggleDelete( )
    -- The bullet has to be removed if it's dead or out of bounds
    if ( self.alive == false) then
        return true
    elseif (( self.y < -20 ) or ( self.y > 500 )) then
        return true
    end
    return false
end
```

```
-- Remove the bullet from the stage
function Bullet:removeMe( )
    self.spriteInstance:removeSelf( )
    self.spriteInstance = nil
end
```

Updating Active Bullets

The way we'll update bullets is quite similar to the way we added and moved our ships. One table will contain all of the bullets in the game, and we'll loop through it each frame to move or update them. Start by initializing an empty bullet table at the top of the game.lua file.

Shooting/game.lua
```
local bullets = {}
```

Like when we coded ships, when we update bullets, we have to loop backward through the table with each update so that we won't miss any updates if we remove bullets while advancing through the list. Begin by moving bullets using the Bullet:move() function, which uses the bullet's speed to update its position. Then check to see whether the bullet should be deleted using toggleDelete(). Use removeMe() to remove bullets that are out of bounds or that have already collided with something; they are not visible and can no longer affect gameplay. This step is where we check the toggleDelete() function to know whether we have to remove the sprite.

Shooting/game.lua
```
-- Updates all bullets in the game
function updateBullets( group )
    -- Loop through all bullets (backwards in case we remove some)
    for i = #bullets, 1, -1 do
        -- Move the bullet
        bullets[ i ]:move( )
        -- Remove inactive bullets
        if ( bullets[ i ]:toggleDelete( ) == true ) then
            bullets[ i ]:removeMe( )
            removeTableRows( bullets, i, 1 )
        end
    end
end
```

Since bullets move and collide only against enemies, their update() function was easy to write. When removing sprites, always remember to remove both the sprite and any instances from the corresponding table. Otherwise, the images could keep showing or the game loop would try to update nonexistent sprites.

Making Units Shoot

With the Bullet class built, we can start making ships shoot. We'll add a small delay to the Unit class so that the player can't shoot continuously. Begin by creating a variable called nextBullet to store this delay.

Shooting/unit.lua
```
-- Initialize the bullet delay counter
self.nextBullet = 0
```

In globals.lua, we'll set variables called BULLET_RELOAD and ENEMY_BULLET_RELOAD that represent the number of frames we'll force units to wait between shots. We use different variables so that we can have a larger delay for enemy ships. Each time through the tick() function, we'll check to see whether the unit can shoot or its weapon is still cooling down before adding a new bullet.

To do this without having to access the unit's variable table from the game scene, write a function called canShoot() that will load the delay value into nextBullet and check it with each frame. The unit can shoot when nextBullet is equal to or less than zero. If the unit shoots, reset the delay to either the player's or the enemy's reload time, depending on the unit's type.

Shooting/unit.lua
```
-- Returns true if the unit can shoot
function Unit:canShoot( )
    -- Check the bullet delay counter is back to 0
    if (self.nextBullet <= 0) then
        -- Reset the counter to the player's reload time
        --   (depending on the unit type)
        if self.type == TYPE_PLAYER then
            self.nextBullet = BULLET_RELOAD
        else
            self.nextBullet = ENEMY_BULLET_RELOAD
                + math.random( ENEMY_BULLET_RELOAD )
        end
        return true
    end
    return false
end
```

We've randomized the enemy bullet delay and made enemy units shoot as soon as they can, which means that we'll add a new enemy bullet to the scene each time the canShoot() function returns true for an enemy ship. To activate the counter, we need to decrement it with each tick(), so add a line to the Player:move() function to do this.

Shooting/unit.lua
```
-- Update shooting
self.nextBullet = self.nextBullet - 1
```

Now that we have our infrastructure in place, we can add player and enemy shooting to the game scene.

When updating the player, check whether the ship can shoot using the canShoot() function. If it can, add a new bullet to the end of the bullets list by calling the Bullet constructor.

Shooting/game.lua
```
-- If the player can shoot, add a new bullet
if ( playerInstance:canShoot( ) ) then
    local newBullet = Bullet( physics, group, imagesheet, playerInstance )
    bullets[ #bullets + 1 ] = newBullet
end
```

To make enemies shoot, we need to loop through all the enemy ships each frame to see whether any of them are able to shoot, calling the Bullet constructor if they can. Since we're already looping through enemies when we move enemies in the updateEnemies() function with each tick(), just add code to that function to enable enemy shooting.

Shooting/game.lua
```
-- Make the enemy shoot
if ( enemies[ i ]:canShoot( ) == true ) then
    bullets[ #bullets + 1 ] = Bullet( physics, group, imagesheet, enemies[ i ] )
end
```

Now check that the program compiles, and your ships will shoot like in the image here.

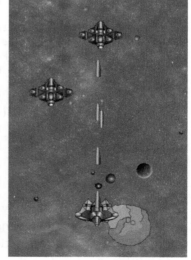

6.3 Checking for Collisions

For bullets to have any effect in the game world, we need a way to check for collisions. We could find them by testing for overlapping pixels in onscreen objects. To do this, though, we'd have to loop through all of the pixels in each object in the game, which wouldn't be efficient. For a simpler and faster check, we could draw a box or circle around each object and then monitor these shapes for overlaps. This technique is known as *bounding box* or *bounding sphere collision checking* and is quite common. Unfortunately, it's not precise for objects with complex shapes.

In Galactic Warfare, we'll use an intermediate solution in which each object is transformed into a polygon of the sort you see in the following figure. This would normally involve applying the *Separating Axis Theorem* and writing a lot of code, but (luckily for us) Corona has an embedded physics engine to check for polygon collisions.

To use Corona's Physics application program-ming interface (API) for collision detection, we need to create a *physics body* for each object on the screen using physics:addBody(). Once this is done, collisions between objects on the screen will trigger a collision event that we can manage with an event listener. To create a physics body, physics:addBody() needs to be passed the shape of the object, which we'll provide as a polygon;

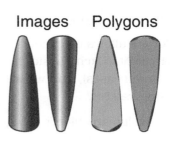

Images   Polygons

some filtering data that determines which other onscreen objects an object should interact with; and what its friction, density, and bounce properties are like.

Object polygons are defined by tables of coordinates, written in the form x1, y1, x2, y2, and so on, that represent their vertices. A 10×10 square, for example, could be passed using { -5, -5, 5, -5, 5, 5, -5, 5 }. Corona would interpret these eight numbers as four sets of x, y coordinates, assigning a 10×10-pixel physics body to the sprite. More complex polygons just imply more vertices. Corona can't handle concave polygons, so concave shapes require dividing objects in two and passing them as two polygons.

The filtering data physics:addBody() is used to tell Corona which objects should interact with one another and which can overlap. As we check for collisions between bullets and ships in Galactic Warfare, for example, the player's ship needs to interact with enemy ships and enemy bullets (but not player bullets), while enemy ships need to interact with the player ship and player bullets (but not enemy bullets). This is done by providing physics:addBody() with some categoryBits for each object that categorize it with other similar objects, and some maskBits to indicate which categories of objects interact with each other and which do not.

It's possible to create physics bodies by defining and entering this data manually, but that's a long and cumbersome process that isn't necessary for successful game development. Instead, most developers use one of a variety of programs to automatically trace bitmaps and then export the generated polygons and related data to Lua. Appendix 1, *Corona Resources*, on page 215, talks about PhysicsEditor and similar tools that simplify the process of creating physics data.

As we implement collisions in Galactic Warfare, we'll rely on the already complete data set I've generated for this chapter using PhysicsEditor, which can be found in shipphysics.lua.

Filtering Collision Checks

Corona allows us to add a filter to physics-engine collisions using maskBits and categoryBits. Each physics body can belong to a category (or multiple categories, in some cases), and we will define the types of categories it will collide with using maskBits.

We assign an object's category by passing a value that is a power of two, such as 1, 2, 4, or 8, up to 2^16, because sixteen is the maximum number of categories compatible with the Physics API. In most cases, we'll group objects of the same type under the same categoryBit. Once we've defined our object's category, we can use maskBits to tell the Physics API which object collisions to check. To do this, we set the variable to be the sum of all of the categoryBits values for the objects whose collisions should be checked. For example, an object that collides with object categories 1 and 2 would need a maskBits property of 3.

Triggering Collision Effects

We'll cause collisions to have consequences—such as destroying a ship or subtracting a life—by using listener functions that will be called whenever a collision takes place. If we wanted, Corona would let us use the same listener function for all of the collisions in the game, but that would require us to check the types of units involved in the collisions and add conditional clauses to react differently to each case. Instead, to simplify our code, we'll add two different listener functions—one to handle collisions with the player's ship and the other to handle collisions with enemy ships.

There are a couple of sticky considerations to keep in mind as we listen for collisions. First, the Physics API iterates to get to its solutions, so a collision listener may be called several times for each collision event. This means removing objects from the stage within a collision listener function can trigger an error. For this reason, we'll delete objects in the Galactic Warfare main game loop rather than in the listeners.

Second, we'll need to be sure to add scores or subtract lives only once for each collision. Since a listener may be called several times before we remove the affected object in the next game tick, we'll perform only the addition and subtraction logic (adding points to the score or subtracting lives) in the "began" event.phase of the listener. We'll maintain a Boolean value called alive for units and bullets, and we'll process collisions only when alive equals true, setting it to false immediately afterward. This process is similar to the one we developed in Planet Defender for our touch listeners.

With our solutions to these problems in mind, we're ready to write playerCollision(), which will be called whenever the player's ship collides with bullets or enemies, and we'll use it to subtract a life from the player and mark the colliding object as destroyed.

We want to perform different actions depending on whether the player has collided with an enemy or a bullet, so check the type of collision that has occurred before acting on it. Then subtract one life when the player's ship collides with a bullet and two lives when it collides with an enemy. Note that we haven't yet implemented game-end conditions, so subtracting lives doesn't affect gameplay; we'll add a function in Section 6.6, *Ending the Game*, on page 105, to end the game once the player has zero lives remaining.

Shooting/unit.lua

```lua
-- Player collision listener function
function playerCollision( self, event )
    -- Get the target object's type
    local other = event.other.object

    -- Only react to collisions if the other unit is alive
    if ( other.alive == true ) then

        if ( other.type == TYPE_ENEMY ) then
            -- Enemy ships subtract a life
            other.alive = false
            lives = lives - 1

        elseif ( other.type == TYPE_ENEMY_BULLET ) then
            -- Enemy bullets subtract a life
            other.alive = false
            lives = lives - 1
        end
    end
end
```

Now that we've created playerCollision() to handle collisions with the player's ship, we can add the listener that will call playerCollision() each time the player ship's physics body collides with those of enemy ships or bullets. To enable the listener to be triggered by Corona's Physics API, we'll also have to add physics bodies to the player's ship and other objects in the game.

Use the physics data found in shipphysics.lua, and an automatically generated get() function that can be found there as well. The get() function accepts a string and looks for a physics body in shipphysics.lua with the same name, retrieving any matching data so that it can be passed to physics:addBody(). I've used the same names for physics bodies in shipphysics.lua that we gave to the sprite frames. This means we can pass physicsData:get() the PLAYER_CENTRE[1] variable, which holds the player sprite's animation name, to retrieve its physics body data.

Add a collision listener by calling sprite:addEventListener() in our constructor, as we did when we added touch listeners. For physics events, however, Corona imposes requirements that are a bit convoluted.

Corona's Physics API will call the collision variable from the parameter we pass to sprite:addEventListener() instead of calling the parameter itself. This means that if we pass instance, Corona will call instance.collision() whenever a collision takes place.

To get Corona to call our playerCollision() function, therefore, set self.spriteInstance.collision as a pointer to the playerCollision() function. We also have to pass self.spriteInstance to addEventListener() instead of directly passing the collision function.

Once we add our listener, it'll be a good time to compile the program to make sure we haven't made any mistakes.

Shooting/unit.lua
```
-- Add the player unit's physics body
physics.addBody( self.spriteInstance, physicsData:get( PLAYER_CENTRE ) )

-- Add the collision listener to the player
local instance = self.spriteInstance
instance.collision = playerCollision
instance:addEventListener( "collision", instance )
```

That's it—player collisions are now active!

We've written collision functions so that they set units' and bullets' alive variables to be false when collisions occur. This means that their toggleDelete() methods, which we always add to objects to check whether they have to be removed, will correctly return true after a player collision takes place. The game loop we've already coded will delete the related objects from the stage as soon as this happens.

We can use the same strategy to detect and handle collisions with enemies. Since we're already handling enemy-to-player ship collisions in the player's collision listener, the enemyCollision() listener function will have to check only for collisions with player bullets. We've defined player bullets as TYPE_PLAYER_BUL-LET in the code on page 90. In the enemy-collision listener function, check whether the collision object is of the TYPE_PLAYER_BULLET type. If it is, set the enemy's alive variable to false.

Shooting/unit.lua
```
-- Enemy collision listener function
function enemyCollision( self, event )
    -- Check the target object's type
    local other = event.other.object
    -- Only process the collision if the other object is alive
    if ( other.alive == true ) then
        -- Player bullets destroy the unit
        if ( other.type == TYPE_PLAYER_BULLET ) then
            other.alive = false
            self.object.alive = false
        end
    end
end
```

The process for adding the collision listener to enemy ships is identical to the process by which we added it to the player's ship. We'll start by setting up a physics body and then add the collision-detection function.

Shooting/unit.lua
```
-- Add the unit's physics body
physics.addBody( self.spriteInstance, physicsData:get( ENEMY_1 ) )

-- Add a collision listener to the unit
local instance = self.spriteInstance
instance.collision = enemyCollision
instance:addEventListener( "collision", instance )
```

The collision listener for enemy collisions is fairly similar to that for players. The only tricky part of collision handling with class instances is remembering to set a pointer to the collision function from instance.collision().

6.4 Adding Animated Explosions

Space battles aren't half as fun if there aren't any explosions, so let's also add some fancy effects to our game now that enemies can be hit by bullets. When a ship is hit, we'll show a basic animated explosion sprite using the images in the sprite sheet in the figure shown here, and then remove it from view as soon as the animation has completed. The explosion sprite was made by Cliff Harris from Positech Games.

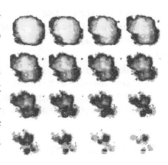

Instead of adding animated sprites directly to the game, we'll build a new class called GameObject and use it to create the animated sprite for explosions. This way it'll be easier to reuse our code later to add other animations and object types to the game.

We'll start with the GameObject constructor. We'll initially create GameObject sprites outside the screen bounds to avoid the brief flicker that can occur as sprite images are displayed before animations begin. Let's design a GameObject so that dynamic sprites that inherit from it automatically add a spriteInstance, saving us the trouble of repeating code for each new kind of object. When we want to display an animation, we'll prepare it, start it, and then move the sprite to its onscreen position.

Shooting/staticsprites.lua
```lua
GameObject = Class( )
-- GameObject constructor
function GameObject:new( group, spriteSet, spriteSequence, px, py )
    -- Create a new sprite and add it to the group
    local spriteInstance = display.newSprite( spriteSet, spriteSequence )
    -- local spriteInstance = sprite.newSprite( spriteSet )
    spriteInstance:setReferencePoint( display.CenterReferencePoint )
    spriteInstance.x = -50
    spriteInstance.y = -50
    group:insert( spriteInstance )
    -- Store the sprite instance and the "self" object
    self.spriteInstance = spriteInstance
    self.spriteInstance.object = self
end
```

Now write toggleDelete() and removeMe() functions similar to the ones we wrote for ships and bullets. Using the same function names across all of our classes makes them easier to remember and cuts down on typos and coding errors (such as calling a method from another class) that Corona won't catch at compile time.

Shooting/staticsprites.lua
```lua
-- Check whether the object needs to be deleted
function GameObject:toggleDelete( )
    return false
end
-- Remove the unit
function GameObject:removeMe( )
    self.spriteInstance:removeSelf( )
    self.spriteInstance = nil
end
```

We now have a GameObject class that we can use to create multiple child classes for easy animations. It uses the same basic toggleDelete() and removeMe() functions that we're already familiar with for deleting objects.

To start implementing explosions, build an Explosion class that inherits from GameObject. Since GameObject adds a new spriteInstance for us and does the necessary work of hiding it outside the screen borders as it's created, all we need Explosion to do is load the correct animation, start it playing, and then immediately position it appropriately on the stage.

Shooting/staticsprites.lua

```
Explosion = Class( GameObject )

-- Explosion constructor
function Explosion:new( group, spriteSet, spriteSequence, px, py )
    -- Prepare the explosion sprite
    self.spriteInstance:setSequence( EXPLOSION )
    self.spriteInstance:play()

    -- Set the sprite's coordinates
    self.spriteInstance.x = px
    self.spriteInstance.y = py
end
```

We need a new toggleDelete() method specifically for explosions that marks them for deletion once their animation has completed so that explosions don't loop continuously. In it, we'll check to see whether the current frame is equal to 25 (the last frame in the explosion animation) and return true if it is. After enhancing toggleDelete(), we'll also add a loop to game.lua to step through ongoing explosions and remove those that have ended.

Shooting/staticsprites.lua

```
-- Check whether the explosion has to be deleted
function Explosion:toggleDelete( )
    -- Delete the sprite if it reaches the final frame
    if ( self.spriteInstance.frame == 16 ) then
        return true
    end
    return false
end
```

Now we need to define the table that will hold the explosion instances currently on the stage. We'll also have to load the explosions sprite sheet independently because it's stored in a different image file. We'll add two variables to the top of game.lua to address these needs—a variable called explosionsheet to hold the sprite set for the explosion animations and a variable called explosions to hold the table.

Shooting/game.lua

```
local explosionsheet
local explosions = {}
```

We'll load the explosion sprites the same way we loaded ship sprites. First require the explosionsprites.lua data file, which contains the explosion sprite definitions, and then use it to load sprites from the image file. Then call sprite.newSpriteSet() to create a new sprite set and call sprite.add() to add the explosion animation to it.

Shooting/game.lua
```lua
-- Load the explosion sprites and create a new sprite set
local eximages = "images/explosionsprite.png"
local explosionOptions = {
    width = 64,
    height = 64,
    numFrames = 16
}
explosionsheet = graphics.newImageSheet( eximages, explosionOptions )
```

To display an explosion, we'll create a new Explosion sprite instance and add it to the end of the explosions table. To do this, we'll pass the constructor the explosions sprite set, the scene group, and the causing bullet's position.

Shooting/game.lua
```lua
-- Add an explosion
local newEx
newEx = Explosion( group, explosionsheet, spriteSequences.explosionSequence,
    bullets[i].x, bullets[i].y )
explosions[ #explosions + 1 ] = newEx
```

Now we have to loop through the explosions table and remove those whose animations have ended. Otherwise, explosions will appear but will never disappear. As before, since we're removing elements from an active table, we'll have to loop backward to avoid skipping elements after an object is removed from the table. The final step is to add a call to updateExplosions() from the game tick().

Shooting/game.lua
```lua
-- Update the explosions
updateExplosions( )
```

That's it. The game tick() function is still neat at this stage, because even though we've added a lot of code to it, we've written it in several functions.

6.5   Adding Power-Ups

Now that we have an expandable GameObject class, let's use it to add power-ups to Galactic Warfare. Power-ups are objects that players "pick up" during gameplay to enhance their ship or obtain a bonus. In this game, we'll cause some enemies to drop power-ups when they die.

Dropped power-ups will appear where the enemy was destroyed and will move downward at a constant speed. If the player collides with a power-up, we'll remove it from the screen and give the player a bonus. If the player doesn't collide with a power-up, we'll just remove it after it moves out of bounds.

We'll keep things simple and add just two power-ups to Galactic Warfare, one that gives the player an extra life and one that enhances the player's "health." For now the second one will be purely decorative, but if we decide to track player health points in addition to lives in a later release of the game, we'll already have the "increase health" aspect of gameplay in place.

To add power-ups, add code for the images we'll use and the speed at which they should move. We can set these parameters in the globals file, just like we did when we defined enemy ship and bullet properties.

Shooting/globals.lua
```lua
-- Power-up variables
POWERUP_SPEED = 4
POWERUPS = {
    HEALTH_POWERUP = "health_powerup",
    PLAYER_LIFE = "player_life"
}
```

In the Powerup constructor, set what type of bonus to offer the player by choosing one at random from the POWERUPS we just added to globals.lua and then retrieve the corresponding animation and physics body. Also create the standard set of variables we've used for our other game objects, including coordinates, type, and alive parameters.

Shooting/staticsprites.lua
```lua
-- Power-up
Powerup = Class( GameObject )

-- Power-up constructor
function Powerup:new( group, spriteSet, spriteSequence, px, py, physics )
    -- Prepare the explosion sprite
    local powerType = math.random( 2 )
    local sInstance = self.spriteInstance
    local body
    -- Set the image and physics body depending on the power-up type
    if( powerType == 1 ) then
        self.spriteInstance:setSequence( POWERUPS.HEALTH_POWERUP )
        body = physicsData:get( POWERUPS.HEALTH_POWERUP )
    else
        self.spriteInstance:setSequence( POWERUPS.PLAYER_LIFE )
        body = physicsData:get( POWERUPS.PLAYER_LIFE )
    end
```

```
    -- Add the body, store the power-up type, and display the image
    physics.addBody( sInstance, body )
    self.type = TYPE_POWERUP
    self.subtype = powerType

    -- Set the power-up's starting parameters
    self.alive = true
    self.x = px
    self.y = py
    self.spriteInstance.x = px
    self.spriteInstance.y = py
end
```

To move a power-up, update the sprite's y position by adding the POWERUP_SPEED that we defined in globals.lua. We want to keep the x-coordinate constant, but we explicitly set it in each frame to ensure that it isn't accidentally skewed by gravity pulls or other collisions in the Corona Physics API.

Shooting/staticsprites.lua
```
-- Move the power-up
function Powerup:move( )
    self.y = self.y + POWERUP_SPEED
    self.spriteInstance.x = self.x
    self.spriteInstance.y = self.y
end

-- Check whether the power-up needs to be deleted
function Powerup:toggleDelete( )
    if self.y > 500 or self.alive == false then
        return true
    end

    return false
end
```

We can check for collisions by adding a few lines to playerCollision() in Unit.lua. Check for the object type TYPE_POWERUP before performing the post–power-up collision logic. Then check the power-up's subtype and either add lives or heal the ship. Though healing the ship doesn't really accomplish anything in this early edition of the game, by adding two power-up types rather than just one, we've forced ourselves to write expandable code that will make new power-up types a breeze in later releases—a great way to keep players happy each time a game update is released.

Shooting/unit.lua
```
elseif ( other.type == TYPE_POWERUP ) then
    -- Power-ups add a life or improve our health
    if ( other.subtype == POWERUP_HEALTH ) then
        self.object.health = self.object.health + 1
```

```
else
    lives = lives + 1
end
other.alive = false
```

That's it—Galactic Warfare now has power-ups! Compile it, and you'll see something like the figure shown here.

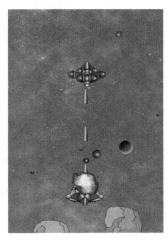

6.6 Ending the Game

Our gameplay still has one glaring omission: there's no way to lose.

It's time to fix that now. To cause the game to end once all of the players' lives have been lost, add a check of the lives variable to see whether it's greater than zero. Any positive number is good, but otherwise call Corona's storyboard:gotoScene() function to return the player to the main menu.

Shooting/game.lua
```
-- Check whether we have some lives left, and return to the menu if we don't
if lives <= 0 then
    storyboard.gotoScene( "menu" )
end
```

6.7 Exercises and Expansion Options

Now that we've finished the chapter, here are a few ideas that you can try to implement if you're feeling adventurous.

Make Enemies Less Random

Enemies in Galactic Warfare appear randomly, so the game will be easier in some instances than in others. Increase the game's difficulty by reducing the time between enemies as the game progresses.

Hint: You can do this by multiplying lastEnemy by a coefficient of less than one. lastEnemy is in charge of setting the number of frames between one enemy and the next. You can gradually decrease the coefficient by multiplying it by 0.95 each time a new enemy appears.

Adding Rudimentary Artificial-Intelligence Behavior

Right now the enemies in Galactic Warfare just move down the screen. This can be both fun and stressful if they appear quickly, but it could also be fun to have them behave in other ways. For example, some enemies could move right or left as they made their way down the screen, or you could create a variable—say, something called movementType—to store whether enemies move right and left, down, or in some other way. You can check this variable in Unit:move() and adjust enemy movement accordingly.

Adding Bosses

Many simple games have harder enemies that appear at some point in the game, and you could also add some of these to Galactic Warfare. You could, for example, design a boss with several hit points that moves to a random location onscreen, pauses for a while, and then shoots once or twice at the player before moving again. Try implementing bosslike behavior for one of your enemy ships. If you're really ambitious, you could make it shoot in several directions or move toward the player in a ship-to-ship attack.

Adding Laser Beams (Challenging)

Though destroying enemies with bullets is fun, laser beams have long been more popular in science fiction. You could expand Galactic Warfare to offer laser beams fired from one ship to another. Remember how we calculated distance in the Planet Defender game? You can use the same CalculateDistance function to measure the distance between the player ship and enemy ships in this game. Ships would shoot a laser beam when they're within a pixel-distance range set in the game globals. You'd want to make the beams appear for a few seconds, so you would have to store them in a table similar to the one in which the current game stores bullets. You can represent the beams using a simple line, as shown in the preceding figure.

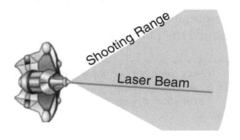

6.8 What We Covered

Before this chapter, we'd used only touch listeners and basic gameplay mechanics, but now we've enhanced Galactic Warfare to the point that it's a fully interactive scrolling and shooting game. We now know how to implement projectile shooting and check for collisions between onscreen units using some basics of the Corona Physics API. We provided the player with opponents that make gameplay challenging and learned to add polish to games with animated explosions and a reusable power-ups class. We also implemented scoring and defeat conditions, making Galactic Warfare reasonably complete.

CHAPTER 7

Adding Sound

Galactic Warfare is relatively complete but lacks sound, and games without sound are boring. While you're completely right that there are no sounds in space, players generally expect to hear explosions and sound effects in space games. Since we don't want them to feel like Galactic Warfare is missing a fundamental component, we'll add sounds to the game. If the players want to be realists, they can choose to disable the sounds.

7.1   What You'll Learn

In this chapter, we'll do the following:

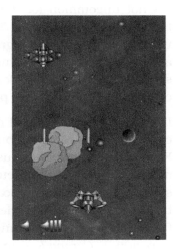

- Learn about the Corona Sound application programming interface (API)
- Add sounds to the game
- Create playlists for background music tracks
- Add volume controls and mute buttons

It's not enough to just add sound effects. It's as important to add them well. Otherwise, we'll be confronted with hordes of angry Galactic Warfare players we've irritated with wrong sound choices, loud sounds, or volumes that can't be changed. A bad review like "One star, needs a mute button!" is a silly way to hurt your app's ratings (not to mention sales) in the app stores. Once we add these changes, our app will look like the image shown earlier.

Since we'll create a few interface elements in this chapter, you'll need to be familiar with the graphics and interface methods we've covered in previous chapters. In particular, before starting this chapter, you might want to give

Chapter 4, *Input and Menus*, on page 55, another look as a refresher on buttons and touch event listeners.

7.2 Finding Game Sounds

Though adding sound does involve programming, we'll first need to find, license, or create music and effects that match the atmosphere and style of our game. This isn't a secondary task; a bad soundtrack or bad sound effects can spoil the entire gameplay experience for our audience.

For sound effects, we'll need sounds of the right tone and length that also complement one another, and we'll need to coordinate their volume levels to avoid inadvertently highlighting some at the expense of others. Explosions shouldn't last for twenty seconds, for example, and bullets ought to make less noise than bombs. It's similarly unhelpful to add very quiet or muffled sound effects to a game, since players may not notice them in the first place.

Similar considerations apply to background music tracks. For a relaxed game, beat-heavy hip-hop music isn't the best choice. Though several music styles might be appropriate within a single game, if they play one after another in sequence, they should complement each other when heard in any order.

It's not uncommon for different sound files to need work before they'll fit together nicely in a game. The easiest solution when sounds need work is to use an audio-editing program to improve them, editing them as necessary and equalizing their volumes appropriately. Fixing sounds in game code by setting different volumes for each sound effect or other similar tricks gets too confusing to be practical, particularly when lots of sounds are involved.

If you prefer to download or buy sounds for your game rather than hire a composer, look to stock sound websites, which are both cheap and effective. For Galactic Warfare we'll use sound effects from SoundBible and background music loops from Incompetech (the game code includes a complete list of our sounds). Soundsnap, AudioJungle, and Soundrangers are also fantastic places to find music with a variety of licenses and prices, while Freesound and freeSFX both offer free sound effects for very tight game-development budgets. Appendix 1, *Corona Resources*, on page 215, lists a few additional resources.

7.3 Understanding the Corona Sound API

Corona, like Flash and other rapid application-development platforms, uses channels to play sounds. Every active channel is a sound or tune that the user can hear. These channels play independently of one another, and we can play a different tune or sound in each of Corona's thirty-two channels.

To add sound effects and background tracks to Galactic Warfare, we'll have to learn how to find an unused channel, start and stop sound playback, and remove completed sounds.

Most of the time, we load sounds using Corona's audio.loadSound() function, which returns an *audio handle*, something like a pointer to the sound in question. After loading sounds, pass their audio handles to audio.play() to play sounds back. In that sense, handles are similar to the sound tools in other development environments and are easy to use in the simplest case, shown here:

SoundPlay/main.lua
```
-- Load and play mysound.wav
mySound = audio.loadSound( "mysound.wav" )
myChannel = audio.play( mySound )
```

Each time we play a sound, Corona assigns the audio to an unused channel ranging from 1 to 32, but we can also tell Corona which channel to use if we want to do so. As long as we know what channel is being used for a sound's playback, we can mute it or change its volume. In Galactic Warfare we'll play all of our background music through one channel (making sure we remember which one it is) and let Corona manage the channels for the rest of our sounds.

7.4 Adding Sound Effects

Now that we know where to find sounds, which sounds to choose, and the basics of sound playback in Corona, we can add sound to Galactic Warfare. Let's begin by adding effects for our shots and explosions so that they can be heard as well as seen, expanding just a bit on the basic sound-playback technique shown earlier.

Loading and Playing Sounds

The basic audio.loadSound() and audio.play() methods shown earlier are fine for a small app with one or two sounds, but what about a big game with dozens of sounds? We could add each sound manually, but that would be a lot more work and involve lots of repeated code, making changes more difficult down the road.

For this reason, we'll use a table to store sound filenames and properties instead and then loop through the table to load each sound and add its audio handle to a table of audio handles.

Begin by listing the audio files for our game in globals.lua using the SOUND_EFFECTS variable. We'll stick to sound effects for now, but we'll do something similar later for background music. The two sound effects we'll use are called explosion.wav and missile.wav and can be found in the chapter's code files.

```
Sound/globals.lua
SOUND_EFFECTS = {
    SOUND_EXPLOSION = "sounds/explosion.wav",
    SOUND_MISSILE = "sounds/missile.wav"
}
```

In addition to the variable listing our sound files, we need a variable to store the sound handles that result from loading them. Using a table will let us access all of our game's sound-effect handles under a single name. First define this variable, calling it something like soundEffectHandles.

```
Sound/game.lua
local soundEffectHandles
```

Now that we have one table listing the files we'll need for sound effects and another one ready to store their handles, we're ready to step through the first table to load the sound effects using audio.loadSound(). Store the handles for each sound in the variable we just defined (soundEffectHandles), and assign names to the table rows so that we can access them by name. Since we're working with explosion and missile sounds, call them explosion and missile.

```
Sound/game.lua
soundEffectHandles = {
    explosion = audio.loadSound( SOUND_EFFECTS.SOUND_EXPLOSION ),
    missile = audio.loadSound( SOUND_EFFECTS.SOUND_MISSILE )
}
```

With our sounds ready to go, let's edit the Galactic Warfare game loop to play a sound effect each time a missile or an explosion is added to the game. We added explosion animations in the updateEnemies() function in game.lua, so we can now call the audio.play() function right after adding the explosion sprite.

```
Sound/game.lua
audio.play( soundEffectHandles.explosion )
```

We can repeat the same steps for the shooting sound. We added bullets using the Bullet() constructor, but the tricky part is that both the player and the enemies can shoot, so we'll have to add bullet sounds twice. We'll start by adding sounds for player bullets, which are created in the game's tick() function. We'll add the audio.play() call there, right after adding each player bullet to the game.

```
Sound/game.lua
local chan = audio.play( soundEffectHandles.missile )
audio.setVolume( 0.1 * gameVolume / 4 , { channel=chan } )
```

We called the enemy update() functions from updateEnemies(), so we'll make our enemy sound changes to game.lua. Add the same audio call right after we add a new enemy bullet to the bullets table. We've used the same sound effect for both player and enemy bullets to keep things simple, so we can use the same code as before.

Sound/game.lua
```
local chan = audio.play( soundEffectHandles.missile )
audio.setVolume( 0.1 * gameVolume / 4 , { channel=chan } )
```

Adding a Mute Button

The sounds we've just added really make Galactic Warfare seem more professional, but there are times when players don't want to hear sound effects. To address this problem, we'll add a mute button using the same technique that we used to add interface buttons to our game menus. To enable muting, we'll add a button and a touch listener for it that will call the muteSounds() function, which we'll use to toggle sound effects on and off.

For the active and inactive mute-button sprites, we'll use the images shown in the figure here. To save time and effort, I've already added to the shipsprites.lua file a mute button and another volume-control image that we'll use later in this chapter. That way we don't have to return to manually adding buttons to our texture definitions or make TexturePacker do it for us.

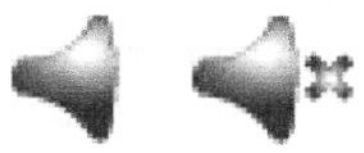

Figure 42—Mute and unmute icons

To get started, create a variable in game.lua called soundEffectsVolume to hold the mute status for sound effects. Set it to true by default, and we'll change the value to false if the player decides to mute the game. We'll also add a soundEffectsImages variable to store the sprite instances.

Sound/game.lua
```
local soundEffectsVolume = true
local soundEffectsImages = {}
```

Before adding the images to the set of sprites in the app, create a table in globals.lua to hold names for the muted and not-muted button images, just as we've done for the other sprites we've used in Galactic Warfare.

Sound/globals.lua
```
FX_MUTE = {
    ACTIVE = "unmute",
    MUTED = "mute"
}
```

After saving the sprite names as global variables, we'll add the mute button to the bottom of the stage. We position it there so that users can quickly tap it without interrupting their gameplay or being distracted by the game. (It's frustrating to lose just after muting sounds.) Players usually want to see the mute button at all times, so adding the buttons to the stage just after creating the scene is a good idea.

Since we don't want to see both images (mute and unmute) at the same time, add both in the createScene() function, but mark one of them as invisible by setting its isVisible property to false. Whenever the player changes the sound settings, we'll toggle the visibilities and make the visible button invisible, and vice versa. Also add a touch listener to the images so that Corona calls a placeholder function called muteGame() when one of them is tapped.

Sound/game.lua
```lua
-- Add an "active sounds" button
local soundsprite = display.newSprite( imagesheet, spriteSequences.soundSequence )
group:insert( soundsprite )
soundsprite.x = 30
soundsprite.y = 450
soundsprite:setSequence( FX_MUTE.ACTIVE )
soundEffectsImages[1] = soundsprite
-- Add a "muted sounds" button
soundsprite = display.newSprite( imagesheet, spriteSequences.soundSequence )
group:insert( soundsprite )
soundsprite.x = 30
soundsprite.y = 450
soundsprite:setSequence( FX_MUTE.MUTED )
soundsprite.isVisible = false
soundEffectsImages[2] = soundsprite
soundEffectsImages[1]:addEventListener( "touch", muteGame )
soundEffectsImages[2]:addEventListener( "touch", muteGame )
```

Now, write the muteGame() function that will mute game sound effects if they're currently active or will enable them if they're currently muted. Remember to toggle the visibilities of the mute and unmute buttons.

Sound/game.lua
```lua
function muteGame( event )
    if event.phase == "began" then
        -- Change the sound FX mute state
        soundEffectsVolume = not soundEffectsVolume
        -- Set visibilities
        if ( soundEffectsVolume == false ) then
            soundEffectsImages[1].isVisible = false
            soundEffectsImages[2].isVisible = true
        else
            soundEffectsImages[1].isVisible = true
```

```
                    soundEffectsImages[2].isVisible = false
            end
            -- Stop all sounds if they're inactive
            if ( soundEffectsVolume == false ) then
                audio.stop( )
            else
                -- Choose another background tune
                chooseNextSong( )
            end
        end
    end
end
```

If you compile the game, you'll be able to see the mute image. If you tap it, it will change to the unmute icon.

Muting Sound Effects

After adding the mute and unmute icons, we have to add their logic. Sounds should not play if sound effects are inactive. Instead of always playing them, we'll first check whether soundEffectsVolume is true. Update the explosion sound effects to add this condition before playing the sound.

Sound/game.lua
```
if soundEffectsVolume == true then
    audio.play( soundEffectHandles.explosion )
end
```

Now do the same for player-bullet effects.

Sound/game.lua
```
if soundEffectsVolume == true then
    local chan = audio.play( soundEffectHandles.missile )
    audio.setVolume( 0.1 * gameVolume / 4 , { channel=chan } )
end
```

Finally, update the enemy-bullet sounds.

Sound/game.lua
```
if soundEffectsVolume == true then
    local chan = audio.play( soundEffectHandles.missile )
    audio.setVolume( 0.1 * gameVolume / 4 , { channel=chan } )
end
```

That's it! Adding a mute button is very quick and easy, and it helps us keep our players happy.

Setting Volume and Properties

Mute and unmute don't need to be our players' only options; Corona also lets us set sound volumes, either for the whole app at once or for individual sound channels.

To add volume controls, we'll use Corona's getVolume() and setVolume() functions. In Galactic Warfare, when users want to change the sound-effects volume, we'll update the volumes for all of the sound-effect channels at once. When users want to change the volume for background music, we'll set the volume for the background music channel.

We'll display volume levels using the same kind of icons that we used for muting, but for volume controls we'll offer four sound levels. Our image options will therefore look like what we see in the figure shown here. As we did for muting, we'll create new sprites, then add them to the stage, and then add the listener functions.

Figure 43—Volume status icons

Start by adding a gameVolume variable to game.lua. For simplicity we'll store volume as an integer from 0 to 3. Corona expects volume requests from 0 to 1, so we'll have to do some division before passing the volume variable to Corona. We'll also add a soundVolumeImages variable to store sprite instances.

Sound/game.lua
```
local gameVolume = 3

local soundVolumeImages = {}
```

As we mentioned earlier, the volume images we need have already been added to the shipsprites.lua code file. With them in place we're ready to store names in globals.lua like we did for the mute-button images. Store a variable, such as FX_VOL, and store the image names (volume_0, volume_1, volume_2, and volume _3).

Sound/globals.lua
```
FX_VOL = {
    "volume_0",
    "volume_1",
    "volume_2",
    "volume_3"
}
```

Now that we've stored the volume-image names in the game, add instances of them to the stage. Once again, do this in createScene() so that the images are added before the players see them. First, we set the visibility of our default image, the one indicating the volume level is set to 3, to true. The remaining sound-level images are inactive, so the visibility is set to false.

```
Sound/game.lua
for i = 1, #FX_VOL do
    soundsprite = display.newSprite( imagesheet, spriteSequences.musicSequence )
    group:insert( soundsprite )
    soundsprite.x = 80
    soundsprite.y = 450
    soundsprite:setSequence( FX_VOL[i] )
    soundsprite.isVisible = false
    soundVolumeImages[i] = soundsprite
end

soundVolumeImages[4].isVisible = true
```

Step through a loop, and assign touch listeners to each of these images. Call a placeholder function called changeVolume() to change the volume no matter which of the three images the player taps.

```
Sound/game.lua
gameVolume = 3
for i = 1, #soundVolumeImages do
    soundVolumeImages[i]:addEventListener( "touch", changeVolume )
end
```

The changeVolume() function will be similar to the muteGame() function we wrote earlier. In changeVolume(), hide the currently active image, and increase the volume level by 1. If the volume is greater than 3, set it back to 1. Then, show the volume image for the new volume level.

```
Sound/game.lua
function changeVolume( event )
    if event.phase == "began" then
        -- Increase volume or reset to 1
        gameVolume = gameVolume + 1
        if ( gameVolume == 4 ) then
            gameVolume = 0
        end

        -- Set visibilities
        for i = 1, #soundVolumeImages do
            if i == (gameVolume + 1) then
                soundVolumeImages[i].isVisible = true
            else
                soundVolumeImages[i].isVisible = false
            end
        end
        audio.setVolume( gameVolume / 4 )
    end
end
```

Deleting Unused Sounds

It's finally time to clean up. At the end of a game, we no longer need our sounds. We can clear the memory they're using as soon as the player exits the game scene by calling the audio.dispose() function from within destroyScene(). We set variable names for our sound handles in globals.lua, and now we'll reuse these handles to delete the sounds. Loop through the soundEffectHandles variable and call the dispose() function for each of them. We'll load them again if the player decides to come back to the game scene and play again.

Sound/game.lua
```
for i = 1, #soundEffectHandles do
    audio.dispose( soundEffectHandles[i] )
end
```

This change will keep our program neat and tidy so that we're not clogging the phone's memory.

7.5 Playing Background Music

In addition to sound effects, most games feature background music loops to make gameplay more enjoyable. We could use the Sound API for shorter music tracks, but loading longer tracks into memory is a no-no since mobile devices tend to have limited memory. Instead, we'll use Corona's Streams API for background music, which opens the files but doesn't load them into memory completely. Fortunately, apart from using different function names, Corona streams code is very similar to Corona sound code.

Loading and Playing Music

As always, we'll store names for our audio loops in globals.lua for easy accessibility. We'll use two background tracks played in sequence forGalactic Warfare, but the steps would be the same no matter how many tracks we had. Store tune1.wav and tune2.wav in a MUSIC variable.

Sound/globals.lua
```
MUSIC = {
    TUNE1 = "sounds/tune1.mp3",
    TUNE2 = "sounds/tune2.mp3"
}
```

Once we've stored the filenames for the tracks, we can declare the variables that will hold their audio handles and channel. In the case of streams, audio handles work like pointers to our current position in an audio track. Declare a variable called musicHandles for the music handles, and declare another one called musicChannel for the channel.

```
Sound/game.lua
local musicHandles
local musicChannel
```

Now call the audio.loadStream() function from createScene(). Call audio.loadStream() for each of the sounds, and store each handle in the variable we've just declared. Once we have initialized these sound variables, we'll be able to start playing them.

```
Sound/game.lua
musicHandles = {
    audio.loadStream( MUSIC.TUNE1 ),
    audio.loadStream( MUSIC.TUNE2 )
}
```

So far, this doesn't change our game's behavior. These changes are just loading the tunes, but we haven't started playing them.

Initializing and Playing Sounds

With Corona's Sound API, we simply used audio.play() to play a sound effect. We'll use the same function with streams to get started, but streams are a bit more complex in that stopping play *pauses* them rather than rewinds them. Subsequent calls to audio.play() will resume the tune from the pause point—which can be unpredictable after multiple plays and stops.

For this reason, we'll use audio.rewind() to rewind the stream before calling audio.play(). To get our tracks to loop, we'll add an audio event listener to the background music channel to call a function that will play another tune each time the previous tune ends.

We can use an event listener called event.completed to notify us when the current stream has finished playing so that we can rewind it and play another one. We'll add the event listener as we create our background channel in createScene(). Start by playing the first tune in musicHandles. Add an onComplete event and call a placeholder function called soundFinished().

```
Sound/game.lua
musicChannel = audio.play( musicHandles[1], {
    channel=1, loops=1, onComplete = soundFinished
} )
```

Now write the function named soundFinished(). First call audio.rewind() to rewind the track that just finished, and then play a new one. For this last step, use a function called chooseNextSong() (that we'll write in the next section) to play a new song from our playlist.

```
Sound/game.lua
function soundFinished( event )
    -- Rewind
    audio.rewind( musicChannel )
    -- Choose another song
    chooseNextSong()
end
```

At this point, we have everything structured so that we can play varied tunes as soon as we write the chooseNextSong() function. In a simpler game with only one music loop, we could just rewind the current tune and play it again and skip the next steps.

Cycling Through Playlists

Write a chooseNextSong() function to start the next song that should be played. We could just pick the next element in our table of songs and keep playing them in sequence throughout the game. If more enthusiastic players devote dozens of hours to our game, however, playing the same tracks over and over again in the same order will get boring very quickly.

To solve this problem, chooseNextSong() will pick a random track from the list of background-music handles we've defined. Use Corona's random() function to pick the song, and then play it and add an onComplete event listener to call soundFinished() once again when the track finishes. The code is very similar to what we wrote to play the first tune.

```
Sound/game.lua
function chooseNextSong( )
    if ( soundEffectsVolume == true ) then
        nextSong = math.random( #musicHandles )
        -- Play the tune and store the ID for the next choice
        currentSong = nextSong
        musicChannel = audio.play(
            musicHandles[nextSong], { onComplete = soundFinished } )
    end
end
```

As it stands now, chooseNextSong() plays a completely random track, which means that an unlucky player could actually hear the same tune over and over again. That can be annoying, too, so instead we'll add a twist to ensure that players never hear the same song twice in a row.

Pick a random number between one and the total number of songs minus one. If the number is lower than the tune we've just played, then play the track with that number. If it's greater than or equal to the number of the tune we've just finished, add one to the number of the next track to be played.

Sound/game.lua
```lua
function chooseNextSong( )
    if ( soundEffectsVolume == true ) then
        -- Choose a song ID without repeating it
        local nextSong
        repeat
            nextSong = math.random( #musicHandles )
        until nextSong ~= currentSong
        -- Play the tune and store the ID for the next choice
        currentSong = nextSong
        musicChannel = audio.play(
            musicHandles[nextSong], { onComplete = soundFinished } )
    end
end
```

Check that the game compiles, and you'll be able to tap the sound icons that appear on the bottom left of the screen, like you can see in the figure here.

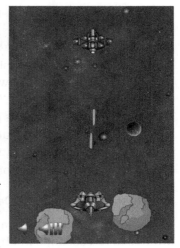

Adding Timed Loops

The program now loops through background music endlessly, regardless of how long players play. Pausing a bit between tracks might be better for the gameplay experience in some games. Let's change the listener to wait a random number of seconds between five and ten before playing another song.

We can use timer.performWithDelay() to add a delay before performing an action. Use it before playing a new tune in soundFinished(). Pass the chooseNextSong() method and a random value between 5,000 and 10,000 milliseconds as the second parameter.

Sound/game.lua
```lua
function soundFinished( event )
    -- Rewind
    audio.rewind( musicChannel )
    -- Choose another song
    local timeDelay = 5000 + math.random( 5000 )
    timer.performWithDelay( chooseNextSong, timeDelay )
end
```

Compile the game, and you'll notice a brief delay after one tune finishes and before another one begins to play.

7.6 Exercises and Expansion Options

Now that we have finished the chapter, here are some ideas you can try to improve this game.

Adding a Sound Settings Panel

Try to add a new panel or scene to enable players to edit their sound settings outside of gameplay. One way to do that would be to copy the scenetemplate.lua file we get whenever we create a new app and then add at least one button to access it from somewhere in our game. In the panel, we'd have to add apply and cancel buttons, as well as an image to tell the player whether sound effects are active. To display that image, we could use the same method we're using to display the images relating to mute status in our game now.

Letting Players Enable and Disable Background Tracks

We've defined a set of music tracks that we continuously loop in the background. Some players, however, might not like one of our tune selections. Maybe they even hate one. They can disable sound or turn the volume down, but that reduces the game's overall quality. Try to add a panel with a checkbox for each of the available tracks so that players can select those they want to hear and disable those they don't want to hear. To do this, check which tunes are active, and pick one from that list each time you play a new tune.

Letting Players Set Music Delay Lengths

We've added a small delay after each music track before the next one begins, but five to ten seconds might be too long a wait for some players and too short a break for others. To address this issue, try to add a slider that players would use to select how long they wanted new tracks to be delayed. You can start by adding the slider to a settings panel and creating a variable for it in the game. When playing new tracks, call timer.performWithDelay() with the value of the user's setting.

7.7 What We Covered

In this chapter, we covered most of Corona's audio functions and applied them to typical game needs. We discussed some of the practicalities involved in choosing and finding sound effects and audio tracks. we talked about how to play these sound effects when game events of our choosing take place. We also saw how to play music continuously during gameplay, how to stop it when players mute it, and how to change audio volume. We explored the differences between Corona's sounds and streams and practiced a few quick tricks to mute sounds selectively and delay their playback.

Part IV

Tower Defense

*We've used sprites in two games so far. Now it's
time to create a more complex project. We'll focus
on making a tower-defense game, with pathfinding,
depth sorting, and saving features. Once we understand all these tools, we'll be ready to create just
about any game project.*

CHAPTER 8

Displaying Maps and Sorting Depths

With Galactic Warfare done, it's time to start a new project: a tower-defense game. For role-playing and strategy-simulation fanatics, this chapter is where the fun begins. In the game we're about to make, players build towers that fight off waves of invading enemies.

8.1 What You'll Learn

In this chapter, we'll work on a new game. To get started, we'll do the following:

- Design the game's map
- Learn how to build towers on the map
- Learn how to set the tower-drawing order so that the towers in the fore-ground appear in front of the others

In Chapter 9, *Adding Movement and Artificial Intelligence*, on page 137, we'll add pathfinding to complete gameplay, and we'll add game-saving features in Chapter 10, *Loading and Saving*, on page 165. By the end of Part IV, we'll have developed a classic tower-defense game, and our app will look like the image shown earlier.

In this project, we'll also focus on writing neater code. To do this, we'll clean up the Lua classes we've used throughout Part II, *Planet Defender*, on page 15, and Part III, *Vertical-Scrolling Shooter*, on page 69, by coding a GameObject class to hold game-related properties like object positions and sprites. Almost every screen object will inherit from it. This strategy helps reduce development time and is essential for staying sane once you're coding larger projects.

8.2 Designing a Tower-Defense Game

In this tower-defense game, enemies will enter a path at one end of the level and try to exit at its other end, while the player builds towers to try to stop them. Since the game can go on for a while, game saves are also important. With that basic description in mind, let's take a look at our goals. We need to implement all of the following:

- A tile-based map
- Tower-building
- Depth sorting (handling overlapping screen objects)
- Shooting
- Enemy pathfinding (logic to keep enemies moving along the path)
- Loading and saving

We'll implement the first three in this chapter. Since these tasks are similar to some we've covered in previous chapters, it'll be easier than it sounds.

8.3 Defining Tile-Based Maps

Up to this point, our game "maps" have been premade backgrounds that scrolled to simulate character movement. For games whose maps influence gameplay, however, each level needs a new map. This would be a lot of work if somebody—probably a very smart person—hadn't invented the concept of tiles.

Using tiles, we can assemble maps on the fly, assigning behavioral properties to each tile. For example, we might define river tiles and wall tiles to be tiles that game units can't cross, while allowing units to move freely over grass tiles. By defining and using game tiles sensibly, we'll also have a framework to build paths, making the process of building functional game maps much easier.

Getting Started

For this project, we'll avoid implementing a game start screen at the beginning. Instead, we'll start with gameplay. As we debug our game, this will save us several seconds with each test by avoiding needless scene transitions. If we were to build the start screen first, stepping past it each time we tested our code would be tedious and annoying, and we'd end up hating our start screen quickly.

Let's create a new storyboard program just as we did in our previous projects. Rename scenetemplate.lua to game.lua and update the storyboard scene name in main.lua so that it loads scenetemplate.lua.

What Are Tile-Based Maps?

Our tile work comes first. Tiles are the regularly sized images that we'll use to make maps, as shown in the following figure.

To make use of them, we divide our map into a grid of tile-sized spaces and then choose a tile for each space in the grid. For a map of rectangular tiles to look seamless to the player, corner tiles need to match the edges of at least two adjacent tiles, border tiles need to match the edges of the surrounding three, and central tiles need to line up with all four tiles around them, one on each side.

Figure 46—A tile set for ground tiles

By arranging and painting our tiles, we'll be able to create large maps with little effort. To keep things interesting, we can create variations on tiles we use most. That way, even if we paint a large area with the same basic type of tile, the map's landscape won't be boring and repetitive. For example, each of the images in the top row of our tile set can be used for the same purpose without worrying about transitions between one tile and the next, and they'll look better when we alternate them than they would if we used a single tile to paint a large area.

We don't have to be artists; we can resort to premade tiles like the ones from earlier in the chapter. They are taken from a site called Lost Garden, and they were made by Daniel Cook.[1]

Using Map-Editing Tools

We could define a variable to store each of the tiles in our map, but that would be a lot of work! For a map 20 rows by 20 columns large, we'd have to write 400 numbers before compiling and testing. It's much easier to use a map editor. With a map editor, we simply load a tile set, create a map visually, and then export it to the program we're writing.

We could write our own map editor, but programs like Mappy, Tiled, or Corona's Lime library already exist and work well, allowing us to load tiles, draw a map, and then quickly implement it in Corona.

---

1. Lost Garden: www.lostgarden.com

There's a sample map level in the chapter's code folders, but you can also work on this chapter using a level of your own design.

In this game, we'll work with a landscape-oriented mobile screen with a standard resolution of 480×320 pixels.

We'll choose to use 40×40 tiles, which amounts to fourteen and a half tiles on the screen horizontally and eight tiles vertically. Rather than try to cut a tile in half, we'll just display twelve horizontally and eight vertically, knowing that it's OK to draw and ignore things outside the screen bounds.

Displaying a Map

Since our tiles are squares with sides of 40 pixels, begin by defining two variables called TILE_WIDTH and TILE_HEIGHT in the globals file.

We could define and use one variable instead of two, but by using two we create more flexible code that can be reused for rectangle-based tiles as well.

DepthSorting/globals.lua
```
-- Tile properties
TILE_WIDTH = 40
TILE_HEIGHT = 40
```

Our tower-defense game won't use scrolling, so our screen-sized grid of twelve by eight tiles will be our map size as well. Code the map as a table, with each row representing a row of tiles.

DepthSorting/tilemap.lua
```
-- tile map
map = {
    { 10, 22, 9, 4, 2, 1, 5, 1, 10, 22, 9, 1 },
    { 10, 22, 9, 5, 2, 1, 1, 2, 10, 22, 11, 16 },
    { 10, 22, 9, 1, 5, 1, 3, 2, 10, 22, 22, 9 },
    { 10, 22, 11, 12, 12, 12, 16, 2, 15, 8, 22, 9 },
    { 10, 22, 22, 22, 22, 22, 9, 1, 1, 10, 22, 9 },
    { 15, 7, 7, 7, 8, 22, 11, 12, 12, 13, 22, 9 },
    { 5, 2, 1, 1, 10, 22, 22, 22, 22, 22, 22, 9 },
    { 5, 1, 3, 5, 15, 7, 7, 7, 7, 7, 7, 14 }
}
```

Since we need to be able to repeat images within the map, we'll load each tile as an individual sprite that we can display as needed. We'll load them as individual sprites using sprite.newImageSheet(). In this method, we simply pass the texture file name (tiles.png), the width and height of each image, and the total images, and Corona does the rest.

```
DepthSorting/tilemap.lua
-- Load the tiles and create a new sprite sheet and set
local options =
{
    width = TILE_WIDTH,
    height = TILE_HEIGHT,
    numFrames = 35,
}
local tileSpriteSheet = graphics.newImageSheet( "images/tiles.png", options )
```

Now we need a way to display the map on the screen. To keep our code neat
and tidy, we'll put map-drawing functions in a file called tilemap.lua. This allows
us to keep similar functions together with one another, organized by file—
which makes reusing game code for future projects much easier. Begin by
creating a function called drawMap() that draws the map on any display group
we pass as a parameter.

In drawMap(), loop through the map table's rows and columns, x-axis tiles (the
variable i) in the inner loop, and y-axis tiles (the variable j) in the outer loop.
For each i, j pair, add a sprite to the group and set its coordinates and current-
Frame variable, which holds the sprite frame to be displayed. Get the tile frame
from the map[y][x] variable.

```
DepthSorting/tilemap.lua
-- Adds the tile map to a group
function drawMap( where )
    for j = 1, #map do
        for i = 1, #( map[j] ) do
            -- Create a new tile image for each table element
            -- and place it in the right position and frame
            local tempImage = display.newImage( tileSpriteSheet,
                map[j][i] )
            tempImage.x = i * TILE_WIDTH - TILE_WIDTH / 2
            tempImage.y = j * TILE_HEIGHT - TILE_HEIGHT / 2

            -- Add the sprite to the group
            where:insert( tempImage )
        end
    end
end
```

Now that tilemap.lua contains the map-drawing code, require the file from
game.lua. Add two layer definitions to the game.lua header, one for the map tiles
and another group where we'll build towers.

```
DepthSorting/game.lua
require( "tilemap" )
mapLayer, towersLayer = nil, nil
```

In the game scene's scene:createScene() function, initialize the two new layers and insert them into the scene's display group. Using two layers allows us to group game objects by layer, which makes displaying foreground and background images much easier. For this game, we want towers to be able to overlap, but we always want them to appear in front of map tiles, so map tiles will go into the background layer.

DepthSorting/game.lua
```
-- Create groups
mapLayer = display.newGroup( )
towersLayer = display.newGroup( )
group:insert( mapLayer )
group:insert( towersLayer )
```

Call drawMap() from the main game scene to draw the map.

DepthSorting/game.lua
```
-- Draw the map
drawMap( mapLayer )
```

If everything worked, you'll see the map on the simulator. A drawn map is shown in the figure shown here.

Figure 47—A tile-based map in Corona

8.4 Building Towers

This tower-defense game needs towers. Otherwise, our helpless players won't be able to defend themselves against the hordes of enemies that we're going to hurl at them. We don't want players to have an unlimited ability to build towers, though, or the game won't be challenging. Keeping this in mind, we'll limit where and when towers can be built. Certain tiles will be able to support new towers, while others won't, and building towers will cost something, meaning that we'll task the player not only with tower-building but with a resource limitation as well.

Adding Build Sites for Towers

Players of tower-defense games expect some control over where they build their towers; that's the basic element of strategy involved. For this reason, we can't just add a set of towers to the map during game development. Instead, we need to code a way for players to tell the game where they'd like to add a tower while at the same time constraining their tower-building according to a clear set of rules. With this in mind, we can brainstorm a bit to come up with some plausible rules and then work on implementing them in our code.

- Rule 1: Towers can't block enemy paths. If they could, gameplay would be too easy and unrewarding.

- Rule 2: Towers can't be built on some tiles. This lets us vary game difficulty with the combination of tiles in each map.

- Rule 3: Only one tower can be built on any tile. This keeps things simpler for us and makes gameplay simpler and more fun as well.

We'll use these rules in our tower-building functions, and we'll end up with a buildable area, as shown here.

On paper, the test for whether a new tower can be built on a given tile goes like this: first, draw the map and add all tiles to a tower-eligible list; then, remove tiles on the enemy path from the list; then, remove all tiles already containing towers. What remains is a list of tower-eligible tiles. To translate

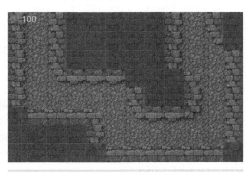

Figure 48—Grid of buildable tiles

this into game code, we'll write a function that makes each of these checks for a single tile, and we'll call it whenever a player chooses a tile and tries to build a tower on it.

To begin, create some variables to store the properties of each type of tile in our tile set. We'll use these variables for each tile so that we know whether units can walk on them. TILE_BUIL indicates a buildable tile, TILE_WALK a path tile, and TILE_EMPTY an unbuildable tile. Set unique numbers to each of them, because we'll use that value as the variable's identifier.

DepthSorting/globals.lua

```lua
-- Tile types (for building and pathfinding)
TILE_WALK = 1
TILE_BUIL = -1
TILE_EMPTY = 0

IMG_GOLD = "currency"
IMG_TOWER = "tower"

-- The cost to build 1 tower
TOWER_COST = 1
```

Let's create a tileProperties table to hold each tile's characteristics. Since the tile set (in the following listing) was laid out as a 5×7 grid, structure the table of tile properties the same way. This makes it easier to match the tiles to buildable properties.

```
DepthSorting/tilemap.lua
-- Stores whether the tiles in tiles.png are walkable
-- or if they can be used to build towers
tileProperties = {
    { TILE_BUIL, TILE_BUIL, TILE_BUIL, TILE_BUIL, TILE_BUIL },
    { TILE_EMPTY, TILE_EMPTY, TILE_EMPTY, TILE_EMPTY, TILE_EMPTY },
    { TILE_EMPTY, TILE_EMPTY, TILE_EMPTY, TILE_BUIL, TILE_BUIL },
    { TILE_BUIL, TILE_BUIL, TILE_EMPTY, TILE_EMPTY, TILE_EMPTY },
    { TILE_BUIL, TILE_WALK, TILE_EMPTY, TILE_EMPTY, TILE_EMPTY },
    { TILE_EMPTY, TILE_EMPTY, TILE_EMPTY, TILE_EMPTY, TILE_BUIL },
    { TILE_EMPTY, TILE_EMPTY, TILE_BUIL, TILE_BUIL, TILE_BUIL }
}
```

Feel free to experiment with tiles' walkable properties and their values. If you ever want to add walkable tiles to slow down enemies, you can add a TILE_SLOW variable and change the movement codes we'll write in the next chapter.

Using a Currency

If we allowed players to build towers until they filled every tower-eligible tile on the map, the game wouldn't be very challenging, and it wouldn't require any strategic thinking. Rather than cap the number of towers a player can build, we'll add a second dimension of strategy to the game by forcing players to buy their towers. Players will start each game with a hundred coins and then earn more for each enemy killed. To do this, declare a variable called playerGold to hold the player's wealth.

```
DepthSorting/moneyfunctions.lua
-- Gold amount
playerGold = 100
-- Text box to show gold amount
goldText = nil
```

To enable tower purchases, create a function called hasEnoughMoneyToSpend() that checks to see whether a player has enough money to buy a tower. Add another function called subtractMoney() to deduct one tower's cost from the player's wealth for each tower built.

```
DepthSorting/moneyfunctions.lua
-- Check we have enough gold, but don't spend it.
function hasEnoughMoneyToSpend( amount )
    if ( playerGold >= amount ) then
        -- The player has enough gold
```

```
        return true
    else
        return false
    end
end

-- Spend gold
function subtractMoney( amount )
    -- Subtract the gold
    playerGold = playerGold - amount

    -- Update the gold text box
    updateGoldDisplay( )
end
```

We also need an addMoney() function to add coins to the player's stash.

DepthSorting/moneyfunctions.lua
```
function addMoney( amount )
    playerGold = playerGold + amount

    -- Update the gold text box
    updateGoldDisplay( )
end
```

We won't use this function yet, but it's easier to code all of our wealth-management functions at the same time. We'll add a call to this function each time an enemy is killed or a level is completed.

Once we add an icon to show the player's gold in the game, it will look something like the figure shown here. This makes it easier to motivate the players to kill the invading enemies.

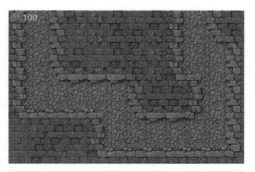

Figure 49—Displaying the player's gold

Tapping to Build Towers

With a simple game like this one, the easiest way to let players build a tower is to have them tap the screen at their desired location. To make this work, add an event listener to game.lua to catch touches during gameplay. Make it trigger a placeholder function called onTouchMap().

DepthSorting/game.lua
```
mapLayer:addEventListener( "touch", onTouchMap )
towersLayer:addEventListener( "touch", onTouchMap )
```

When the player taps the screen, make onTouchMap() calculate which tile the player has touched by dividing touch coordinates by the tile's height and width. Use this to call a placeholder function named checkValidBuildTile() to make sure that there isn't already a tower on the chosen spot and that enemy paths won't be blocked by the tower's placement. Finally, it checks the player's cash balance, builds the tower, and subtracts funds.

DepthSorting/towerbuilding.lua

```lua
function onTouchMap( event )
    if ( event.phase == "ended" ) then
        -- Calculate tile coordinates
        local tileX = math.ceil( event.x / TILE_WIDTH )
        local tileY = math.ceil( event.y / TILE_HEIGHT )
        -- Build only if the tile is valid and we have enough money
        if checkValidBuildTile( tileX, tileY ) and
                hasEnoughMoneyToSpend( TOWER_COST ) then
            -- Subtract the money and build the tower
            subtractMoney( TOWER_COST )
            buildTower( tileX, tileY )
        end
    end
end
```

We need checkValidBuildTile() to return true if the player can build on the tapped tile, and false otherwise. Start by using the x and y values we receive in check-ValidBuildTile() to get the tile type for the tile in question, which is at map[y][x].

DepthSorting/towerbuilding.lua

```lua
function checkValidBuildTile( x, y )
    -- Get tile type
    local tileType = map[y][x]
    -- Get the tile type's buildable property
end
```

Once we know what type of tile the player wants to build on, check the tile properties table to see whether a tower can be built on that tile. Remember that we used a properties table with five tiles per row? Divide the tile type by five to get the position in the tile properties table. Since we don't want to use decimal numbers, use ceil() to round up the result. Then check the buildType list, which gets us the tile type at each position.

DepthSorting/towerbuilding.lua

```lua
-- Get location in the tileProperties table
local setCoordX = 1 + (tileType - 1) % 5
local setCoordY = math.ceil( (tileType) / 5 )
-- Get the tile build / walk type
local buildType = tileProperties[setCoordY][setCoordX]
```

Now that we know the buildType for the tile the player has selected, we can compare it against the rules that we outlined earlier and the TILE_BUIL variable. If the tile's buildType is TILE_BUIL, then we know the player can build on the selected tile. Before returning true, however, we also need to check whether the tile contains an existing tower. For this, we need a new table, towersInMap. This variable will store a 0 for empty cells and a pointer to the tower sprite if there's a tower.

DepthSorting/towerbuilding.lua
```
-- Check whether a tower can be built on this tile
-- We can only build on this tile if it's a TILE_BUIL tile
if ( buildType == TILE_BUIL ) then
    -- Return true if there are no towers in this tile
    -- print( "buildable" )
    return ( towersInMap[y][x] == 0 )
else
    -- print( "not buildable: " .. tileType .. ", " .. buildType )
    return false
end
```

We still need to define the towersInMap table that we just used to see whether the [y][x] position was equal to 0. Create it at the start of the game and set it to 0 for each tile, which means that the tile is empty. As towers get built, we'll update the table to contain references to tower objects. Then we'll know not to build two towers on the same spot, and we'll be able to quickly edit or access the properties of any particular tower.

DepthSorting/towerbuilding.lua
```
function clearTowersInMap( )
    -- Loop through all the map's tiles, and initialize towersInMap to 0
    towersInMap = { }
    -- For each column
    for j = 1, #map do
        -- Initialize a list with values of 0 for each row
        towersInMap[j] = { }
        for i = 1, #( map[j] ) do
            towersInMap[j][i] = 0
        end
    end
end
```

With this change, we only need to build the towers, and we'll be ready to go.

Building the Towers

It's finally time to implement tower-building. There is a catch, though. Players will tap where they want the *base* of a tower to be, but our tower images are many pixels tall. If we allow Corona to use the center of the tower's image as a reference point and to place that reference point at our coordinates, the tower's bottom will appear below the player's tap on the screen, making gameplay more confusing and less immersive. To fix this, we need to adjust either the coordinates that we use (offsetting them from the tap) or the Corona reference point for each tower.

To build towers, adopt the second approach, choosing the bottom center of each tower (the center of the image's lower bound) as its reference point. That way, the tower's base is placed at the coordinates where the player has tapped. To create a tower, add a sprite, and then set its reference point and coordinates accordingly before inserting it. Make sure to update the towersInMap variable to avoid building two towers on the same spot.

DepthSorting/towerbuilding.lua
```lua
function buildTower( x, y )
    -- Create a new tower sprite
    local tempSprite = display.newImage( imagesheet,
        spritedata:getFrameIndex( IMG_TOWER ) )
    tempSprite.currentFrame = 1
    tempSprite:setReferencePoint( display.BottomCenterReferencePoint )
    tempSprite.x = x * TILE_WIDTH - TILE_WIDTH / 2
    tempSprite.y = y * TILE_HEIGHT

    -- Add the sprite to the group and store it in towersInMap
    towersLayer:insert( tempSprite )
    towersInMap[y][x] = tempSprite

    -- Sort depths
    sortTowers( )
end
```

That's it! Compile the game and test the building code.

8.5   Sorting Depths in Corona

So far we've used groups in Corona to simulate layers of the kind seen in graphics programs like Photoshop. In Galactic Warfare, for example, we worked with an explosions layer, a ships layer, and an asteroids layer to ensure that asteroids were behind ships and explosions were in front of everything else. In Tower Defense, however, dozens of buildings and units need to be able to overlap in ways that give the impression of depth. In practical terms, we need a sound approach to depth sorting.

Swapping Sprite Depths and Sorting Towers

Without good depth sorting, in a game with the perspective we're using for Tower Defense, the playing area can quickly begin to look disorganized. For example, one tower might incorrectly appear in front of another.

We'll avoid this problem by using Corona's object:toFront() function, which brings an object to the topmost layer within its group. Our rule for a game with square map tiles will be that onscreen objects with higher y coordinates should always appear *in front of* objects with lower y coordinates.

With this in mind, loop through the towers, from lowest y-coordinate to highest, and use object:toFront() to push each building to the front. After looping through the towers on the stage, the ones that were pushed to the front earliest will be the farthest back, with later towers obscuring any earlier ones that they overlap.

DepthSorting/towerbuilding.lua
```
function sortTowers( )
    for j = 1, #map do
        for i = 1, #( map[j] ) do
            if ( towersInMap[j][i] ~= 0 ) then
                -- Tower found! Push it to the front
                towersInMap[j][i]:toFront( )
            end
        end
    end
end
```

This method of depth sorting might seem a bit messy, but it gets the job done, with relatively simple code. Take a look at the result in this figure.

8.6 Exercises and Expansion Options

Now that we have finished the chapter, here are some ideas you can try to improve this game.

Upgrading and Selling Towers

Figure 50—Displaying towers in the right order

Adding tower upgrades and selling can make the game even more fun. Upgrade and sell buttons can appear whenever the player taps a tower. Choosing them will trigger tower-upgrading and -selling options. Tapping outside the tower's area of influence would make the buttons disappear again.

Adding Several Tower Types

Having one type of tower certainly does the job, but we can enhance gameplay by expanding the code to include an array of tower types with different properties and costs. This adds another strategy element to the game but also requires us to implement code to allow the player to select from among several towers after tapping a buildable tile.

Changing Tower Costs

Right now all of our towers cost the same amount, but tower-defense games are strategy games, and players would have to be more strategic if tower costs weren't fixed. We can improve gameplay by updating the game's code to increase tower costs as the number of towers increases.

8.7 What We Covered

In this chapter, we covered how to create map-based games using tiles and how to correctly sort depths so that the display order of game objects makes sense. We implemented a basic game framework and added tower-building functions and their associated gold-management functions. This chapter's skills give us a framework for creating maps for 2D games. After discussing pathfinding Chapter 9, *Adding Movement and Artificial Intelligence*, on page 137, and achievements in Chapter 11, *Physics and the Accelerometer*, on page 183, we'll be able to make games that are even more complex than this.

Adding Movement and Artificial Intelligence

Let's continue working on the tower-defense game. In this chapter, we'll add enemies and enemy movement to the map we previously created. This is one of the most rewarding parts of game-making, since it's fun to debug a program with moving enemies. There's also a danger: getting addicted to playing our own game instead of working on it. Let's hope this won't happen to us!

9.1   What You'll Learn

In this chapter, we'll do the following:

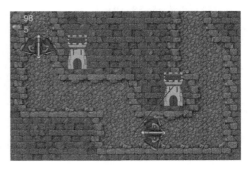

- Add enemy sprites
- Implement enemy movement
- Learn how to make enemies follow paths by using the Dijkstra and A* pathfinding algorithms
- Add shooting to towers
- Show health bars above enemy sprites
- Add loss conditions: enemies that aren't killed before reaching the end of the map will take a life from the player

By the end of the chapter, our app will look like the image shown earlier.

9.2   Adding Enemies

Without enemies to fend off, building towers isn't all that much fun, so it's time to create an enemy class using the custom class we've used throughout the book. Let's build an Enemy class that maintains variables for an enemy unit's coordinates, speed, direction, and health. It will also need an alive variable so that we know whether a unit is alive or dead.

Pathfinding/enemy.lua

```lua
Enemy = Class( )

-- Constructor
function Enemy:new( position, group, creepData )
    -- Create a new sprite and add it to the group
    local spriteInstance = display.newImage(
        imagesheet, spritedata:getFrameIndex( IMG_ENEMY ) )
    spriteInstance:setReferencePoint( display.CenterReferencePoint )
    -- self.coordinates = { spriteInstance.x, spriteInstance.y }
    self.speed = creepData.speed
    self.direction = 0
    self.health = creepData.hp
    self.maxHealth = self.health
    self.bounty = creepData.moneyPerKill
    self.alive = true
    self.spriteInstance = spriteInstance
    self.spriteInstance.object = self

    -- Create a group and insert the sprites in it
    self.unitGroup = display.newGroup( )
    group:insert( self.unitGroup )
    self.unitGroup:insert( spriteInstance )
    self:drawHealthRect( )
    self:updateHealth( )

    -- Coordinates
    self.x = position.x
    self.y = position.y
    self.unitGroup.x = position.x
    self.unitGroup.y = position.y
    self.targetX = self.x
    self.targetY = self.y
    self.spriteInstance.x = 0
    self.spriteInstance.y = 0

    -- Find a path from the spawn point to the exit point
    -- Calculate the path
    self.path = findPath( math.ceil( position.x / TILE_WIDTH ),
        math.ceil( position.y / TILE_HEIGHT ), endTile.x,
        endTile.y, group )
end
```

Now we'll need the toggleDelete(), move(), and removeMe() functions, which are very similar to their counterparts from previous chapters. The toggleDelete() function will check the alive variable. When enemies exit the scene or are killed, alive will indicate this, and removeMe() can then remove the sprite. The move() function will move the units along the path.

Pathfinding/enemy.lua

```lua
-- Movement
function Enemy:move( )
    -- Move the unit using the speed and angle
    self.x = self.x + self.speed * math.sin( self.direction )
    self.y = self.y + self.speed * math.cos( self.direction )
end

-- Check whether the unit should be deleted
function Enemy:toggleDelete( )
    if (( self.y < -20 ) or ( self.y > 340 )
    or ( self.x < -20 ) or ( self.x > 500 )) then
        -- The unit is out of bounds
        return true
    elseif self.alive == false then
        -- The unit is dead
        return true
    end

    -- Alive
    return false
end

-- Remove function
function Enemy:removeMe( )
    self.spriteInstance:removeSelf( )
    self.spriteInstance = nil
    self.rectangleForeground:removeSelf( )
    self.rectangleForeground = nil
    self.rectangleBackground:removeSelf( )
    self.rectangleBackground = nil
    self.unitGroup:removeSelf( )
    self.unitGroup = nil
end
```

We won't use these functions just yet. Instead, we'll use them once we've started adding creep waves.

Defining Creep Waves

In our other games, we generated enemies randomly and didn't vary their fighting intensity over time. Variable intensity keeps players involved and on their toes while also giving them some time to recover. After all, we don't want any heart attacks. Tower-defense games are great for experimenting with enemy waves because adding rest time isn't boring "nonplay" time. Instead, players take advantage of breaks to build and maintain their towers.

In tower-defense games, enemies are called *creeps*, and they always come in intimidating waves that increase in intensity as levels progress. We'll keep creep waves simple in our game and define them in a table called enemyWaves. Write each table row to store information about the type and number of creeps to come in a wave, their speed, hit points, and the delay between one creep and the next.

Pathfinding/creeps.lua

```
-- Enemy waves: creep type, speed, hit points, number of creeps,
--   spawn delay, and gold per kill
enemyWaves = {
    { 1, 4, 10, 10, 100, 5 },
    { 2, 4, 15, 8, 70, 5 },
    { 3, 2, 20, 6, 30, 10 },
    { 4, 4, 10, 30, 25, 6 },
    { 1, 1, 100, 1, 50, 50 }
}
function getNextWaveData(wave)
    -- Get current wave data
    local enemyWave = enemyWaves[wave]
    creepData = {
        type = enemyWave[1],
        speed = enemyWave[2],
        hp = enemyWave[3],
        number = enemyWave[4],
        spawnDelay = enemyWave[5],
        moneyPerKill = enemyWave[6]
    }
end
getNextWaveData( 1 )
```

Having fleshed out the waves of creeps, we'll add a timer to the game, both to tell players when the next wave will begin and to help us keep track of when to spawn the next creep. Having a timer in place will also help us debug and polish the game. We can use the timer to evaluate how long waves last, how long it takes us to kill the creeps, and whether our wave durations are appropriately challenging. Begin by adding a delay variable to hold the timers' values.

Pathfinding/creeps.lua

```
nextEnemySpawn = creepData.spawnDelay + 30
nextWaveSpawn = creepData.number
spawnedEnemies = 0
```

The timer will check the delay variable in the game's tick() function, spawning a new creep when the timer runs out. To implement spawning, begin with a set of offscreen spawnCoordinates from which enemies will emanate.

Decrease the delay timer each frame. Once it hits zero, add a new creep to the game. We spawn a creep by passing the spawnCoordinates to the constructor, which creates the unit and sets its initial location, and then we reset the next-EnemySpawn counter to the timer delay value to start the cycle again.

Pathfinding/creeps.lua

```
function addEnemies( group )
    -- Add new enemies periodically
    nextEnemySpawn = nextEnemySpawn - 1
    if ( nextEnemySpawn == 0 ) then
        enemies[#enemies + 1] = Enemy( spawnCoordinates, group, creepData )
        nextEnemySpawn = creepData.spawnDelay
        -- print( creepData.spawnDelay )
        spawnedEnemies = spawnedEnemies + 1
        -- Check if the wave ended
        -- print( spawnedEnemies .. ", " .. nextWaveSpawn )
        if ( spawnedEnemies == nextWaveSpawn ) then
            spawnedEnemies = 0
            level = level + 1
            -- print( "level: " .. level )
            getNextWaveData( 1 + level % #enemyWaves )
            adjustDifficulty( level )
        end
    end
end
```

Accounting for Player Skill

Skilled players have a knack for reaching the end of games or perfecting their skills and ending up bored. Our resources are limited, so we don't want to add reams of levels to the game if only a small percentage of players will ever see them, but we also don't want the best players to experience repetitive gameplay or a game-ending "you won" screen just because they're great tower-builders.

To keep the game interesting for good players, we'll add advanced levels using an easy trick. Once all of the initial levels have been beaten, we'll jump back to the first level but multiply the level settings (the number of creeps, their health, and so on) by coefficients that intensify gameplay. Start by storing coefficients to increase the number of creeps in a wave and their health points.

Pathfinding/globals.lua

```
-- How much the difficulty increases for each block of levels
-- Parameters: number of creeps, health
gameDifficultyIncrease = { creepMultiplier = 1.5, healthCoeff = 2 }
```

We also need to update the code where we set level parameters to make use of this change. The variable levelRound will hold the number of times the player has reached the "final" level.

Each level's difficulty is set by multiplying levelRound by our coefficients.

Pathfinding/creeps.lua
```
function adjustDifficulty( level )
    -- Adjust the level round if we've looped through all the levels
    local levelRound = math.ceil( ( level + 1 ) / #enemyWaves )

    -- Adjust the level's parameters based on the current level round
    creepData.spawnDelay = math.ceil( 1 + creepData.spawnDelay /
        ( levelRound * gameDifficultyIncrease.creepMultiplier ) )
    creepData.number = levelRound * gameDifficultyIncrease.creepMultiplier
    creepData.hp = levelRound * gameDifficultyIncrease.healthCoeff
end
```

That's it. This is a very simple change, but it makes the game less static. Ten minutes of work can create endless hours of fun for players.

9.3 Implementing Enemy Movement

Enemies in our previous games moved in straight lines, but in Tower Defense our players will expect enemies to follow paths. To meet this expectation, enemies will need to find their way around a map. This is called *pathfinding*, and it makes enemies seem much smarter.

To begin to implement pathfinding, first update the enemy-creation code to call a placeholder function named findPath(). Newly added enemies will use it to generate a path. Since the path isn't supposed to change, we can call it only once and forget about it. In other games, we'll have to call the pathfinding function whenever the walkable terrain is updated.

Pathfinding/enemy.lua
```
-- Find a path from the spawn point to the exit point
-- Calculate the path
self.path = findPath( math.ceil( position.x / TILE_WIDTH ),
    math.ceil( position.y / TILE_HEIGHT ), endTile.x,
    endTile.y, group )
```

Now create a framework to enable enemy movement along an already determined path. Let's create a new Enemy:move() function that gets called once for each enemy from the game's tick() routine.

Each tick, Enemy:move() will move a creep toward the next set of target coordinates along its path. To have enemies orient themselves (rotate) toward coming coordinates as they move, use sines and cosines like we did in Planet Defender. When a unit reaches its target location, its movement pauses until the next tick(). Once we implement the pathfinding functions, they'll take care of updating a creep's target coordinates to match the next node on its path so that movement continues seamlessly with each tick().

Now call this function from the tick() function so that all enemies move.

Pathfinding/creeps.lua
```
-- Move enemies in the game
function moveEnemies( )
    -- Loop through all enemies
    for i = #enemies, 1, -1 do
        local enemy = enemies[i]
        enemy:move( )
    end
end
```

We don't have a pathfinding algorithm implemented yet, but we have a framework to follow paths after they're calculated. The next step is—you guessed it—to calculate these paths.

Finding Paths with Brute Force

The easiest and most intuitive way to find the best path across a map is to test each and every possible route. Brute force is computationally unfeasible in larger games, but it's a nice introduction to pathfinding in smaller games. We'll start with brute force as a learning exercise and then optimize our approach later in the chapter. The brute-force method we'll use to test all possible paths is called *Dijkstra's algorithm*, and though it's not commonly used for games for efficiency reasons, seeing how it works will make more advanced algorithms easier to understand.

Using the Dijkstra approach, we'll calculate the distance from a start tile to every other tile on the map. We need three tables of information to make it work. First, a distances table will hold the shortest distance, if known, from the start tile to every other tile. Next, a "previous tile" table will hold the previously discovered tile along the path leading to any given tile. Finally, a "currently open tiles" table lists all the tiles adjacent to those for whom we already have distances on file. After all, since each of these will be only one tile away from a tile with a known distance, we'll be able to quickly calculate distances for these adjacent "open tiles" as well.

We'll use pathCost to hold the distances table, previousTile to hold references to the last tile we stepped on to get to each tile, and openNodes to hold the list of open tiles. We call it *path cost* because it's the classic term for distance used in pathfinding. Tiles are called *nodes* in this algorithm, so we'll use both names interchangeably.

First initialize the pathCost table to contain values of -1, indicating that we don't know the distances to any tiles yet. Then do the same with the previousTile table, indicating that we don't know any paths between tiles yet.

Pathfinding/pathfinding.lua

```lua
-- Prepare our program to implement the pathfinding algorithms
-- Initialize a list of open nodes and set the current node
local currentNode = { startX, startY }
local openNodes = { currentNode }
local start = { startX, startY }
local destination = { endX, endY }

-- Create travel times (path cost) and previous tiles lists for
--     the whole map and set their values to -1 (unvisited)
local pathCost = { }
local previousTile = { }

for i = 1, mapHeight do
    pathCost[i] = { }
    previousTile[i] = { }
    for j = 1, mapWidth do
        pathCost[i][j] = -1
        previousTile[i][j] = -1
    end
end

pathCost[startY][startX] = 0
```

With this foundation laid, we can implement findPath(). Begin by passing start and end tiles and then set the pathCost variable for the start tile to 0, since that's the one distance we know at the outset (there is no distance to travel from the start tile to itself). We then add the start tile to openNodes and begin to loop.

While we have open tiles, calculate the distance to the first tile's neighbors (four of them most of the time or less than four if it's a border tile). If there's no distance yet listed for a tile, store the distance we've just calculated. If there is a distance already listed (meaning that we've already found another path to that tile), compare the distances. If the new distance is shorter, the algorithm has found a better path, so replace the existing distance with the new one, and the existing previousTile reference with a reference to the current open node. Whenever the program finds a distance it didn't have before or replaces a longer distance with a shorter one, add the referenced tile to the openNodes list to loop through it in future iterations.

Each time through the loop, check the next tile in the openNodes list and process the four tiles adjacent to it. Continue to loop until there are no more open tiles in the list, meaning that we have found the best paths from the start tile to any other tile on the map, including the destination.

Pathfinding/pathfinding.lua

```lua
-- Find paths using Dijkstra
function findPath( startX, startY, endX, endY, group )
    -- Initialize arrays
    -- Loop until we scan all the map
    local loops = 1000
    repeat
        loops = loops - 1

        -- Get the next open node
        currentNode = openNodes[1]

        -- Get the current node's neighbors
        local neighbors = {
        { currentNode[1] - 1, currentNode[2] },
        { currentNode[1], currentNode[2] - 1 },
        { currentNode[1] + 1, currentNode[2] },
        { currentNode[1], currentNode[2] + 1 }
        }

        -- Loop through the neighbors
        --    and add unvisited ones to the open list
        for i = 1, #neighbors do
            local neighbor = neighbors[i]

            -- Check this is a valid tile
            -- Find paths if the tile is within bounds
            --    and it is walkable
            if (neighbor[1] > 0) and (neighbor[1] <= mapWidth)
                and (neighbor[2] > 0)
                and (neighbor[2] <= mapHeight)
                then

                -- Calculate the new path cost
                local prevCost =
                    pathCost[currentNode[2]][currentNode[1]]
                local newCost = prevCost + 1
                local currentCost =
                    pathCost[neighbor[2]][neighbor[1]]
                -- Update the path cost for new tiles
                -- Or if the new cost is less than the previous cost
                if currentCost == -1 or newCost < currentCost then
                    pathCost[neighbor[2]][neighbor[1]] =
                        newCost
                    previousTile[neighbor[2]][neighbor[1]] =
                        currentNode

                    -- Add the tile to the open nodes list
                    openNodes[#openNodes + 1] = neighbor
                end
```

```
        else
            if (neighbor[1] > 0) and (neighbor[1] <= mapWidth)
                and (neighbor[2] > 0)
                and (neighbor[2] <= mapHeight) then
            end
        end
    end

    -- Remove the previous node from the list
    removeTableRows( openNodes, 1, 1 )
until (#openNodes == 0) or (loops < 0)

-- Check whether we found a path
end
```

Since tiles in Tower Defense are also marked walkable or not walkable, we have to take this into account and build paths that adapt to the map. Instead of adding all unvisited adjacent tiles to the open list, only add walkable tiles (those that have the TILE_WALK property), and ignore any others. To implement this change, check the tile type before adding new tiles to the open nodes list.

Pathfinding/pathfinding.lua

```
-- Find paths if the tile is within bounds
--    and it is walkable
if (neighbor[1] > 0) and (neighbor[1] <= mapWidth)
    and (neighbor[2] > 0)
    and (neighbor[2] <= mapHeight)
    and getWalkableType( map[neighbor[2]][neighbor[1]] ) == TILE_WALK
    then

else
    if (neighbor[1] > 0) and (neighbor[1] <= mapWidth)
        and (neighbor[2] > 0)
        and (neighbor[2] <= mapHeight) then
    end
end
```

Once looping is complete and the list of distances is ready, we can loop backward through the tiles and find the shortest path starting from the destination tile. Since we stored a little cheat for each tile that points to the previous one in its path (previousTile), we can easily build a tile list for the enemy path. Begin with the last tile in the shortest path, identify its previous tile and then that tile's previous tile, and so on, until we get to the start. Return the full list of tiles as the discovered path. The path will look something like Figure 52, *Dijkstra's algorithm: results*, on page 147.

Now we can use this basic pathfinding implementation for Tower Defense.

Figure 52—Dijkstra's algorithm: results

Pathfinding/pathfinding.lua

```lua
-- Check whether we found a path
if (map[destination[2]][destination[1]] ~= -1) then
    -- Path found! Return it.
    local path = { destination }
    currentNode = destination
    print( currentNode[1] .. ", " .. currentNode[2] )

    -- Loop through the tiles until we reach the start of the path
    while ( currentNode[1] ~= start[1] )
        or ( currentNode[2] ~= start[2] ) do

        showPathCost( currentNode[1], currentNode[2], "x", group )
        currentNode = previousTile[currentNode[2]][currentNode[1]]
        path[#path + 1] = currentNode
    end
    path[#path + 1] = start
    showPathCost( currentNode[1], currentNode[2], "x", group )

    -- Path found!
    return path
else
    -- No path found
    return {}
end
```

In Enemy:move(), enemies move until they have reached their target coordinates. To make this happen, we need to update this code to have enemies use successive tiles from the path list as their next set of destination coordinates. If and when they reach the end of their path, mark them as victorious and deduct one of the player's lives.

Pathfinding/enemy.lua

```lua
function Enemy:move( )
    -- Calculate the x and y distances to the target
    local dx = self.targetX - self.x
    local dy = self.targetY - self.y
    local hypotenusesq = dx * dx + dy * dy

    -- print( hypotenusesq )
    -- If we're close to the target coordinates, get the next target tile
    if hypotenusesq < 100 then
        -- print( "path: " .. #(self.path) )
        if #(self.path) == 0 then
            -- The unit reached the end of the path. It wins.
        else
            -- Get the next tile
            local destinationPos = self.path[#(self.path)]
            self.targetX = ( destinationPos[1] - 0.5 ) * TILE_WIDTH
            self.targetY = ( destinationPos[2] - 0.5 ) * TILE_HEIGHT
            dx = self.targetX - self.x
            dy = self.targetY - self.y
            self.direction = math.atan2( dy, dx )
            self.spriteInstance.rotation = 90 +
                self.direction * 180 / math.pi
            removeTableRows(self.path, #self.path, 1)
        end
    end

    -- Move the unit
    -- print( self.direction)
    -- print( self.direction )
    self.x = self.x + self.speed * math.cos( self.direction )
    self.y = self.y + self.speed * math.sin( self.direction )
    self.unitGroup.x = self.x
    self.unitGroup.y = self.y

    -- print( self.spriteInstance.rotation * 90 )
end
```

Since we update the desired direction and target coordinates whenever an enemy reaches the next node in the path, units now move correctly across the map. In comparison to the reasoning behind it, the code isn't all that complicated. It is, however, inefficient; it would be nice to have a better pathfinding algorithm for slow devices or for future games with larger maps. If we don't take the walkable-tile limitation when looking for paths like in Figure 53, *Calculated tiles using Dijkstra*, on page 149, this method calculates every tile.

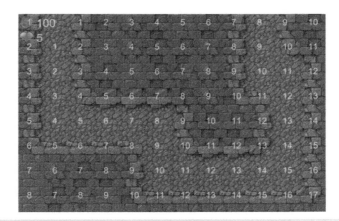

Figure 53—Calculated tiles using Dijkstra

Optimizing Paths: Adding A* Algorithms

The *A* algorithm* is similar to Dijkstra's algorithm but focuses on finding one path to the target destination and stops calculating as soon as it finds it. It does this by estimating the distance from each tile to the target and then combining this estimate with distance to identify paths.

For A*, in addition to distances and preceding tiles, we'll add a table to hold *heuristic* (estimated) numbers that guess how long the remainder of the path to our destination is likely to be. That way, we can predict the shortest path without having to visit all of the game's tiles first as we did using Dijkstra. In the A* implementation, for each open tile we process, we'll add its distance from the start to the predicted distance remaining to the destination. Instead of choosing the next tile in the open-tiles list each time through the loop, we'll choose the one with the lowest predicted total path (as shown in Figure 54, *Traveled (top) and predicted (bottom) path costs in A**, on page 150).

Once again, pathCost holds the distance to the current tile, pathPrediction holds the predicted distance to the end of the path, and openNodes and closedNodes hold the tiles we haven't visited and those we've already visited, respectively. We track closedNodes because for A* we might have to recalculate closed nodes (in other words, the nodes for which we've already calculated path lengths) if we find a shorter path from one of the newly visited tiles. The pathPrediction variable is just the sum of x and y differences because it's the minimum distance a unit will travel from each tile until it gets to the end point.

First, define pathCost, pathPrediction, openNodes, and closedNodes as empty tables. Then, loop through each tile and set pathCost to store values of -1 (not visited)

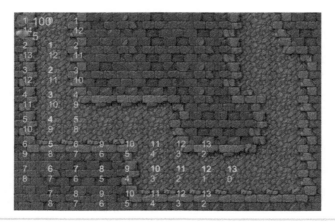

Figure 54—Traveled (top) and predicted (bottom) path costs in A*

for each tile. Calculate the minimum distance it will take to reach the end, and store it in pathPrediction. Finally, set the pathCost of the start tile to 0 because it doesn't take time to travel to the starting point.

```lua
-- Variables for the cost, path predictions, and nodes
local currentNode = { startX, startY }
local openNodes = { currentNode }
local start = { startX, startY }
local destination = { endX, endY }
local pathCost = {}
local pathPrediction = {}
local previousTile = {}
-- Initialize the prediction and cost variables
for i = 1, mapHeight do
    pathCost[i] = { }
    previousTile[i] = { }
    pathPrediction[i] = { }
    for j = 1, mapWidth do
        -- The cost is -1 until we reach this tile in the algorithm
        pathCost[i][j] = -1
        previousTile[i][j] = -1
        -- The prediction is dx + dy
        local dx = math.abs(endX - j)
        local dy = math.abs(endY - i)
        pathPrediction[i][j] = dx + dy
    end
end
-- Set the start tile's cost to 0
pathCost[startY][startX] = 0
```

Pathfinding/pathfinding-astar.lua

In the pathfinding code, begin with the start tile again, adding nodes to the open list as you loop through open nodes. Unlike we did in the brute-force experiment, we stop as soon as we find a path to the end point or run out of open tiles, which means we can't visit any new neighboring tiles and can't get to the destination.

With each loop, calculate the distance from the tile to each neighboring one, and calculate the sum of their distance and the remaining distance prediction (pathCost + pathPrediction).

To choose a new open node in each iteration, select the one with the lowest predicted total distance. Finding paths this way saves us time (the major benefit of the A* algorithm) but doesn't necessarily find the shortest possible path. Since a slightly longer path won't affect gameplay for most games, A* is often a good choice.

Pathfinding/pathfinding-astar.lua
```lua
-- Loop until we find a path or run out of open nodes
local loops = 50
repeat
    loops = loops - 1
until (#openNodes == 0) or (pathCost[endY][endX] ~= -1) or (loops < 0)
```

By enhancing the Dijkstra algorithm code, we've found a way to calculate enemy paths using the more efficient A* algorithm. Our enemies in Tower Defense now have fast, tile-type-aware pathfinding.

9.4 Adding Tower AI

The towers in Tower Defense don't do anything yet, so our enemies still move freely without fear of attack. We can't allow that, can we? It's time to make towers shoot at nearby enemies to stop them from reaching the end of the path and hurting the poor player.

Tower-defense games adopt a variety of approaches to have towers shoot at enemies. Some have them shoot at the nearest enemy, some have them shoot at the enemy farthest along the path, and others lock on to a target creep and shoot at it until it moves out of range or dies. This last option is probably the most fun, since it makes towers seem smarter. Rather than randomly weakening the whole wave, towers that work this way will focus on and try to kill one enemy at a time.

Let's start coding for this shooting model by adding a variable called target to the Tower class. That way, towers can choose a target and remember it, and we won't change a tower's target unless the unit dies or moves out of range.

Pathfinding/tower.lua
```lua
-- Store the enemy target
self.target = 0
```

Now call Tower:update() from the game's tick() function to update targets for each tower every frame. Since towers don't get removed in Tower Defense levels, we can loop from start to end for a change. If the Tower:update() function returns a valid target, call a placeholder function called shootProjectile(), which we'll implement shortly to have the tower shoot.

Pathfinding/tower.lua
```lua
function updateTowers( )
    -- Update the towers each frame
    for i = 1, #towers do
        local target = towers[i]:update( enemies )
        -- If the tower returns a target, shoot a new bullet
        if target ~= 0 then
            shootBeam( towers[i], target )
        end
    end
end
```

Tower:update() has to do two things. If a tower isn't targeting anything yet or its last target has died or moved out of range, it finds a new target. If the tower is able to shoot, then the reload counter will be reset to add time between shots. Let's start by coding the general structure of the function.

Pathfinding/tower.lua
```lua
-- Make the towers aim and shoot at enemies
-- Return an enemy target if we're shooting; 0 if we're not.
function Tower:update( enemies )
    -- Update reload count
    self.reload = self.reload - 1
    -- Only update if we're able to shoot
    if self.reload <= 0 then
        -- Check if we have a valid target
        if ( self.target == 0 ) or ( self.target == nil )
            or ( self.target.alive == false )
            or ( CalculateDistance( self, target ) > self.range ) then
            -- The previous target isn't valid. Look for a new target.
            -- ...
        else
            -- Keep shooting at the current target
            self.reload = self.reloadTime
            return self.target
        end
    end
    -- We're not shooting.
    return 0
end
```

Now, let's move on to the code where the current target is not valid. In this part, we'll reset the current target because it's no longer necessary. Then, we'll loop through existing enemies to look for the closest target. If we find a good target, we'll return it.

Pathfinding/tower.lua

```
-- The previous target isn't valid. Look for a new target.
self.target = 0
if #enemies > 0 then
    -- Loop through the list of enemies
    --   to find the nearest target
    -- ...

    -- Check whether we found a good target
    -- ...

end
```

Within this code, the first step is to loop through the enemies and find the closest one. Start by setting a distance variable to store the closest enemy's distance to the tower and setting a pos variable to keep track of the closest unit. Within the loop, just calculate the distance to each unit. If the distance we've just calculated is lower than the distance variable, then we update both distance and pos so that the tower will target that unit instead.

To check for shooting range, calculate the x- and y-coordinate differences, find the hypotenuse of the triangle, and compare it to the tower's maximum shooting range. Here, I'm calling a CalculateDistance() function that I've written in an auxiliary code file because we've already calculated distances in previous games. You can use this function if you download the book's code files, or you can salvage some of our previous code or write it from scratch.

Pathfinding/tower.lua

```
-- Loop through the list of enemies
--   to find the nearest target
local pos = 0
local distance = 99999999
for i = 1, #enemies do
    -- Ignore dead enemies
    if ( enemies[i].alive == true ) then

        -- Calculate the distance
        --   to the enemy
        local tempDistance =
            CalculateDistance( self,
                enemies[i] )
        -- Compare to current distance;
        --   store the smaller value
```

```
        if tempDistance < distance then
            distance = tempDistance
            pos = i
        end
    end
end
```

At this stage, we've already chosen the closest target. If the closest enemy is out of range, we won't lock on yet, but of course we'll try again the next frame; once the enemy is in range, the shooting can begin! Here, I'm using a variable called reloadNotShoot, which we can set to 1 or any other number so that towers don't keep trying to shoot every frame if they don't find any enemies.

Pathfinding/tower.lua
```lua
-- Check whether we found a good target
if ( pos > 0 ) and ( distance < self.range ) then
    -- We found one! Let's shoot at it.
    self.target = enemies[pos]
    self.reload = self.reloadTime
    return self.target
else
    -- We didn't find any targets
    --  reset the reload counter
    self.reload = self.reloadNotShoot
end
```

Once we know that towers can shoot, we have to decide how to make them shoot. Two easy options are to implement bullets or laser beams. Bullets need time to hit their targets, and beams are almost instant. Since we already worked with bullets in the previous chapter, let's take a look at how laser beams work.

Shooting Laser Beams

Now we need to implement the shootBeam() function, in which we draw a new laser beam (line) from the tower to the target. We'll need the beam's starting and ending positions, so we'll pass those to the Beam constructor. We also have to subtract a health point from the enemy creep, so let's call a placeholder updateHealth() function, and we'll write it later.

When a tower shoots and the program calls the shootBeam() function, add a new Beam instance to a bullets array we'll use to hold active bullets.

Pathfinding/tower.lua
```lua
function shootBeam( tower, target )
    target:updateHealth( 1 )
    beams[ #beams + 1 ] = Beam( beamsLayer,
        tower.x, tower.y - 40, target.x, target.y )
end
```

Laser beams are very fast, so we're not going to draw their movement. Instead, we'll draw them fully formed, and we'll remove them after a few seconds have passed. Loop through the game's laser beams, update them, and remove any beams that can be removed. You can encapsulate this code using methods called toggleDelete(), update(), and removeMe() instead of writing everything explicitly right now.

Pathfinding/beam.lua
```lua
-- Update the beams
function updateBeams( )
    for i = #beams, 1, -1 do
        -- Update the beam
        local beam = beams[i]
        beam:update( )

        -- Delete inactive beams
        if ( beam:toggleDelete( ) == true ) then
            beam:removeMe( )
            removeTableRows( beams, i )
        end
    end
end
```

Laser beams are easier to update than bullets. Instead of updating a beam's position, update its life function. We'll use that to check whether a laser beam is still active. If the life is less than zero, make sure that toggleDelete() returns true so that removeMe() can remove the image from the stage.

Pathfinding/beam.lua
```lua
-- Subtract 1 frame from the active counter
function Beam:update( )
    self.life = self.life - 1
end

-- Check if a beam is alive
function Beam:toggleDelete( )
    if ( self.life <= 0 ) then
        return true
    end

    return false
end

-- Remove a beam
function Beam:removeMe( )
    self.beam:removeSelf( )
    self.beam = nil
end
```

Now it's time to write the Beam constructor. The basic tasks in this constructor are to draw a line representing the laser beam and to set its initial life. You can draw a line on the screen by using the display.newLine() function and passing its start and end coordinates. Use setColor() to change its default color.

Pathfinding/beam.lua

```lua
-- Beam class
Beam = Class( )

-- Beam constructor: create a blue line
function Beam:new( group, startX, startY, endX, endY )
    local beam = display.newLine( startX, startY, endX, endY )
    beam:setColor( 0, 0, 200 )
    beam.width = 2
    beam.antialias = true
    group:insert( beam )
    self.beam = beam
    self.life = 8
end
```

Once you have finished the beam constructor, laser beams are ready to be used. They'll be really fast and hit any enemies that fly past them. You can tweak your game's settings to decide whether you want towers to have a limited range or whether they can shoot at everything on the screen, as shown in the following figure.

Figure 55—Laser beams

Displaying Enemy Health Bars

While it's certainly fun to see enemies die, skilled players will also want to know how much life each enemy has left. To show that, we'll add a simple health bar to foes so that players can manage enemies and tower-building more strategically.

Some games create fancy images for health bars and update them as units are hit. Others add a transparency to units, making them less and less opaque as they get closer to death. Many do what we're going to do: use simple colored rectangles to indicate health, as you can see in the following figure.

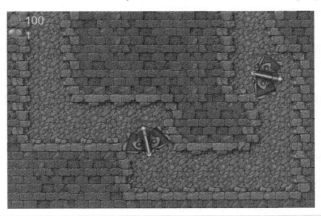

Figure 56—Ship health bars

Corona can draw rectangles using display.newRect(), which takes a rectangle position and size as parameters. Health bars will consist of two rectangles: a background rectangle showing the "full health potential" of a creep and a foreground rectangle of a different color, drawn over it, that shows the unit's actual health value.

Create a new function called Enemy:drawHealthRect() to draw both rectangles and add both of them to a group. This enables units and their rectangles to move together, without our having to update rectangle positions ourselves.

Pathfinding/enemy.lua

```
-- Draw the health rectangles
function Enemy:drawHealthRect( )
    -- Draw the background rectangle (grey with transparency)
    local rectangleBG = display.newRect( -HEALTH_BAR_WIDTH / 2, -35,
        HEALTH_BAR_WIDTH, HEALTH_BAR_HEIGHT )
    rectangleBG:setFillColor( 200, 200, 200 )
    rectangleBG:setReferencePoint( display.CenterLeftReferencePoint )
    rectangleBG.alpha = 0.5
    -- Draw the foreground rectangle (red)
    local rectangleFG = display.newRect( -HEALTH_BAR_WIDTH / 2, -35,
        HEALTH_BAR_WIDTH * ( self.health / self.maxHealth ),
        HEALTH_BAR_HEIGHT )
```

```
rectangleFG:setFillColor( 150, 50, 50 )
-- Set the reference point to the left to be able to scale it afterwards
rectangleFG:setReferencePoint( display.CenterLeftReferencePoint )
-- Add both bars to the enemy's group
self.unitGroup:insert( rectangleBG )
self.unitGroup:insert( rectangleFG )
-- Store the rectangles for quick access
self.rectangleBackground = rectangleBG
self.rectangleForeground = rectangleFG
end
```

It's not enough to simply draw two rectangles; we also have to update the foremost rectangle's size with every frame. We can use the Corona object.xScale property to do this. Our red rectangles have a maximum width of HEALTH_BAR_WIDTH. While this width is nonzero, the unit is alive. When it reaches zero, the unit is dead.

Pathfinding/enemy.lua

```
function Enemy:updateHealth( amount )
    -- Subtract amount and add gold to the player
    if ( amount ~= nil ) then
        self.health = self.health - amount
        if ( self.health <= 0 ) then
            addMoney( self.bounty )
            self.alive = false
        end
    end
    -- Update the health bar's width
    self.rectangleForeground.xScale = self.health / self.maxHealth + 0.01
end
```

Now creeps have their health bars above their heads. This will help us balance gameplay more easily during debugging, since it's easier to see whether enemies are too easy or too hard to kill. This change will also give players a chance to use *creative language* of various kinds whenever a creep reaches the end of the labyrinth with the tiniest bit of health remaining.

Killing Enemies

We've implemented health bars but not enemy deaths, so enemies keep moving even with no health left. We've already written a function called toggleDelete() that tells us when we're supposed to remove enemies, so let's update the moveEnemies() function so that it removes inactive enemies.

As you loop through each unit, check whether it should be deleted using its toggleDelete() function, and remove it from the table and call its removeMe() function to delete it. Remember that we have an auxiliary handy function in arrayfuncs.lua that lets us remove a Lua table row by calling removeTableRows().

Pathfinding/creeps.lua

```lua
-- Move enemies in the game
function moveEnemies( )
    -- Loop through all enemies
    for i = #enemies, 1, -1 do
        -- ...
        -- Remove inactive enemies
        if ( enemy:toggleDelete( ) == true ) then
            enemy:removeMe( )
            removeTableRows( enemies, i )
        end
    end
end
```

Now that the app checks to see whether units should be dead and kills them off when this is so, gameplay is almost complete. We can use this change to go back and optimize our levels. Now that some enemies are removed before making it across the whole screen, we can better calibrate the number of enemies that ought to spawn in each level.

Decreasing the Players' Lives

Players' towers can now knock enemies out of the game, but if players don't strategize well, a few enemies will still reach the end of the level's path from time to time. We have to implement code to decrease player lives when this happens. Since it doesn't make much sense to keep victorious enemies in the game, we also need code to remove them.

Update the Enemy:move() function so that whenever the unit reaches the end of its path, the program marks it as dead and removes a life from the player. Once you update the number of lives, call a placeholder function called updateLivesDisplay() so that players get visual feedback once they lose lives.

Pathfinding/enemy.lua

```lua
function Enemy:move( )
    -- If we're close to the target coordinates, get the next target tile
    if hypotenusesq < 100 then
        -- print( "path: " .. #(self.path) )
        if #(self.path) == 0 then
            -- The unit reached the end of the path. It wins.
            self.alive = false
            lives = lives - 1
            updateLivesDisplay( )
        else
            -- Get the next tile
        end
    end
end
```

The next step is to display those lives. You can draw a heart (using the IMG_LIVES frame if you're using this chapter's code files) and add a text box beside it so that it displays the player's lives. You can create this text box by using the display.newText() function and customize its color using the setTextColor() function. Make sure to call this function from the game. Otherwise, the lives won't be displayed.

Pathfinding/gamelogic.lua
```lua
-- Show the number of lives that the player has
function showLives( group )
    -- Add an image to display the life
    local lifeIcon = display.newImage( imagesheet,
        spritedata:getFrameIndex( IMG_LIVES ) )
    lifeIcon:setReferencePoint( display.TopLeftReferencePoint )
    group:insert( lifeIcon )
    lifeIcon.x, lifeIcon.y = 4, 28

    -- Add a text box
    livesText = display.newText( group, lives, 28, 28, 100, 20,
        native.systemFont, 18 )
    livesText:setTextColor( 255, 200, 200 )
end
```

It's easy to update lives using a text box because we need to access only its text property.

Pathfinding/gamelogic.lua
```lua
-- Display the player's lives
function updateLivesDisplay( )
    livesText.text = lives
end
```

Now when our enemies reach the end of a level's path, we remove them and subtract a life. Players finally have to try their best to stop enemies from reaching the end of the path, and our game is ready to come to an inevitable end once enemy waves are too hard for the player to handle. You can see the result in Figure 57, *Showing lives in the game*, on page 161.

Adding a Game-Over Scene

We're ready for game-over conditions now, so we'll monitor the player's remaining lives in the tick() function. When player lives drop below zero, we'll tell Corona's Storyboard API to jump to the game-over screen.

Pathfinding/game.lua
```lua
-- Check game over conditions
if ( lives <= 0 ) then
    storyboard.gotoScene( "gameover" )
end
```

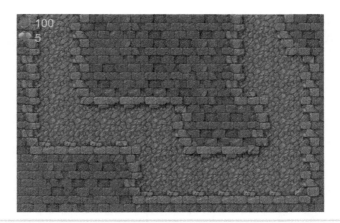

Figure 57—Showing lives in the game

Our simple game-over scene will display an image that says "Game Over."
You can use game_over.jpg, which uses interface elements designed by Lamoot
at OpenGameArt, from the chapter's code files. The final addition, a touch
listener, will take players back to the main menu when they tap the game-
over image. Add it with a delay using timer.performWithDelay() to avoid accidental
taps during the scene transition.

Pathfinding/gameover.lua
```lua
-- Touch event listener for the menu's background image
-- Goes to the game scene
local gotoGame = function( event )
    -- Only process the event if the player started the tap
    if ( event.phase == "began" ) then
        storyboard.gotoScene( "game" )
    end
end


-- Adds the event listener
function addListener( event )
    bgimage:addEventListener( "touch", gotoGame )
end

-- Called when the scene's view does not exist:
function scene:createScene( event )
    local group = self.view

    bgimage = display.newImage("images/game_over.jpg")
    group:insert( bgimage )

    timer.performWithDelay( 2000, addListener )
end
```

You can compile the game and check that the game-over image appears once players lose all their lives. Your game will look like the following figure.

Figure 58—The game-over image

9.5 Exercises and Expansion Options

Now that we have finished the chapter, here are some ideas you can try to improve this game.

Different Creep Types in Each Wave

At this point, each level in our game uses only one creep type to attack the player's defenses. It can be more challenging to use two or three enemy types per level. To implement this change easily, divide the level definition table into two: one for levels and another for enemies. The enemies table can be in charge of displaying enemy properties, and the levels table can hold level details and a list of enemies that will appear in each level.

Changing Level Parameters

In this chapter, we updated our level data to include tougher and more frequent enemies when the player is revisiting a level. However, that's a bit radical and can lead to exponential difficulty increases for some of the levels and too little change in others. For example, level 1 will usually be very simple in most games, so we'll need to make it a lot more difficult with high coefficients. However, level 10 might be quite hard in itself, so doubling the number of enemies might render it impossible. Fix this by updating the level definition tables to use unique difficulty coefficients rather than a gamewide set of values.

Adding Different Terrain Types

We can add a variable called WALK_SLOW to globals.lua to allow for the inclusion of tiles that slow movement. Working with different tile speeds will require a change to the A* pathfinding algorithm that adds a meaningful path cost instead of a cost of one for each nearby tile. We also have to change creep-movement speeds to be appropriate to the tile speed each time a creep enters a new tile.

9.6 What We Covered

In this chapter, we added enemy units to our game to keep our towers from seeming useless. We implemented enemy pathfinding and movement; Tower Defense now behaves like a classic tower-defense game, and players can play it to an unlimited number of levels (assuming they're skillful enough).

In the next chapter, we'll finish Tower Defense by adding loading and saving features. This will increase our app's replay value and keep players coming back for more. It'll make our game much better because replay value is exactly what we want if we opt to add in-game advertising.

CHAPTER 10

Loading and Saving

Our apps so far have allowed players to start, play, and then close a game. However, if the player came back and wanted to play again, the game didn't remember anything about the last session. One of the easiest changes that we can make to enhance the challenge and entertainment value of our games is to remember player scores or statistics across gaming sessions.

10.1 What You'll Learn

In this chapter, we'll use Corona's SQLite and File I/O application programming interfaces (APIs) to implement loading and saving options. We'll do the following:

- Learn how to open, create, read, and close files
- Access folders so that our games can manage their files neatly
- Create SQL databases and tables
- Use SQL queries to track player stats

The best part of this chapter is that we'll use persistent storage, so we'll be able to keep track of player stats over multiple game starts and stops. By the end of this chapter, our app will look like the figure shown earlier.

There aren't many prerequisites to starting this chapter, since files and databases are relatively independent topics in Corona. We will, however, build on the Tower Defense game we've been developing in the past couple of chapters, so it's a good idea to review Part IV, *Tower Defense*, on page 121, and get an overview of the structure of the game (if you don't already know it) before beginning this chapter.

10.2 Loading Levels

We can get a good introduction to Corona's file-management tools by storing levels in external files. That way, levels will be editable with external programs, and we avoid having to recompile and export our games each time we make map changes, something that will save us considerable development time.

Opening and Closing a File

We can open files in Corona by calling io.open(), naming the file to be opened and the access mode (read-only, append, or write modes using "r", "a", or "w", respectively). We need to pass a valid path, since many mobile devices won't let us open or write files just anywhere. We can get Corona to help us build a path by passing a filename and a desired folder type (a documents folder or resource folder, as shown in the following table) to system.pathForFile(). Using io.open() and system.pathForFile() together, we'll always be able to open text files.

System Folder	Description
system.ResourceDirectory	Use this to go to the app's installation folder (to access images or sounds). Don't add files to this folder during runtime!
system.DocumentsDirectory	Store files here to use them indefinitely.
system.TemporaryDirectory	Store files here that won't be needed after the game closes.
system.cachesDirectory	Store files here to save game statuses from one app launch to the next.

Begin by using system.pathForFile() to get the path to levels.txt in the device's app-installation directory. Use this path to open the file in read-only mode, and store its handle in a variable.

```
LoadingAFile/main.lua
-- Get the path to the file in the documents folder
local fullPath = system.pathForFile( "files/levels.txt", system.ResourceDirectory )

-- Open the file in read mode
local fileHandle = io.open( fullPath, "r" )
```

Refer to Table 1, *File Open Modes*, on page 167, for a description of the different modes for opening a file.

After attempting to open a file, we have to check to make sure there were no errors before using read() to start reading it. That's why we saved the second variable output by io.open() as errors.

File Open Mode	Description
"r"	Read mode. Starts reading at the beginning of the file.
"w"	Write mode. Overwrites existing files and starts writing at the beginning.
"a"	Append mode. Starts writing at the end of a file without changing its contents.

Table 1—File Open Modes

Make sure you copy levels.txt to the application folder. Then, call print() and fileHandle:read() to write the text file's contents on the console. Once you're done with it, close it by calling io.close(). If there were errors opening the file, you can use print() and pass the errors variable as a parameter. That will help you debug the issue.

```
LoadingAFile/main.lua
-- If we've opened it, read it
if ( fileHandle ) then
    -- Read it and print it on the console
    print( fileHandle:read("*a") )
    print( "Successfully read the file!" )
end

-- Close the file
io.close( fileHandle )
```

At this point, our program opens the file and prints its content to the console. This can be very useful for game development to check whether level files are written properly or to make sure at times that we're reading the right file.

Storing Game Levels in Files

With file input and output basics under our belt, let's think about how to use these concepts for our game. To make external level files really worthwhile, we want them to hold enough information to enable more or less complete level development to be done without recompiling. With this in mind, we'll structure our files to include the following:

- The map
- Enemy types and numbers for this map
- Enemy spawn locations for this map

These three variables can be used to represent just about any level we might want for Tower Defense.

Now we have to decide how to organize this information to make it easily readable by our game. For large game projects, we could develop a separate WYSIWYG level-editor app that automatically exports formatted level files. We could even devise ways for level creators to test them before playing them in the game. For Tower Defense, however, we'll use simple text files, which are easy to parse.

Let's start by creating a file called level.txt. Write section headers for each kind of data we want to include. Add some spacing between sections in the file to make editing easier, as we can ignore any extra spaces when we read the files.

Since we're using Lua, let's stick to the -- commenting convention for any lines that we want the parser to ignore, such as the section headers. Write a map title and then add two sections to represent map data and enemy data.

LoadingAndSaving/files/level.txt
```
-- Level name: Level 01
-- Map Data: width * height, followed by the map rows
-- Spawn coordinates and end coordinates
-- Enemy Data: creep type, speed, hit points,
--     number of creeps, spawn delay, and gold per kill
```

Now that the headers are ready, we can start to add level data to them, beginning with a table of the map's tiles. First, add integers for the width and height of the map in tiles (12 and 8 in this case). This is a bit redundant in Tower Defense because we're using fixed-sized maps, but it's good planning in case we ever expand the game to allow for multiple map sizes. After describing the map's width and height, add rows of tiles by writing the tile numbers for each of the tiles, laying them out in a table, as shown in the following code example.

LoadingAndSaving/files/level.txt
```
-- Map Data: width * height, followed by the map rows
12 8 -- Width and Height
10 22 9 4 2 1 5 1 10 22 9 1
10 22 9 5 2 1 1 2 10 22 11 16
10 22 9 1 5 1 3 2 10 22 22 9
10 22 11 12 12 12 16 2 15 8 22 9
10 22 22 22 22 22 9 1 1 10 22 9
15 7 7 7 8 22 11 12 12 13 22 9
5 2 1 1 10 22 22 22 22 22 22 9
5 1 3 5 15 7 7 7 7 7 7 14
-- Spawn coordinates and end coordinates
2 1
10 1
```

For enemy definitions and spawn points, use the same layout we used when coding the game. Enter one set of enemy parameters (in other words, the type of enemy, the number of enemies, and the frame delay between enemy spawns) per spawn point, writing the number of spawn points in before the rest of the data so that we know how many points to load.

LoadingAndSaving/files/level.txt
```
-- Enemy Data: creep type, speed, hit points,
--     number of creeps, spawn delay, and gold per kill
2 -- Number of spawn points
1 4 10 10 100 5
2 4 15 8 70 5
```

We also need a separate map of levels to store the order in which to load level files. We could use numbered names like level01.txt through level25.txt, but that could create extra file-renaming work when adding or deleting levels. Instead, we'll keep a list of level files in levelMap.txt. This file tells the game what levels to load and in what order they're to be loaded. Once the game can read these files, adding, editing, removing, or changing the number of levels in the game will require only a quick update to level files.

In this file, type the number of levels, followed by the filenames to load.

LoadingAndSaving/files/levels.txt
```
1 -- Number of levels
level01.txt
```

Reading Level Files

We know how make level files, and we've saved the level map as a text file as well. Let's update the game's level-definition code so that it loads levels from external files instead of using hard-coded values. Start by loading the level list into a table at the beginning of game.lua.

First, open levels.txt using io:open(). Since we're accessing files we'll distribute with our game app, use the app's resource directory by calling system.pathForFile() and passing both the filename and the folder (in this case, system.ResourceDirectory). Since we're reading only the file, pass the I/O mode "r" as the second parameter to io:open(), and store the file handle in a variable called fh.

LoadingAndSaving/loading.lua
```
-- Get the path and open the file from the resource directory
local fullPath = system.pathForFile( "files/levels.txt", system.ResourceDirectory )
local fh = io.open( fullPath, "r" )
```

With the file open, we can read it using the newly created file handle. Use file:read() to get the number of levels to load. Remember that we can pass a parameter to the read() function to tell it how to read each line. Read each of the level filenames by calling a placeholder function called LoadLevelInfo(). We can preload all of the levels in Tower Defense because there isn't that much information in them. If the game were more complex, we'd load one level at a time to avoid overloading the program or the device.

LoadingAndSaving/loading.lua
```lua
-- Get the number of levels
local numLevels = fh:read( "*n" )
fh:read("*l")

-- Initialize Level Data
levelMaps = { }
creepInfo = { }
spawnPos = { }

-- Load each of the level files
for i = 1, numLevels do
    local levelName = fh:read("*l")
    loadLevelInfo( levelName )
    -- Store the level in the game's level array
    levelMaps[i] = tileMap
    spawnPos[i] = spawnPoints
    creepInfo[i] = creepData
end
```

Now, implement LoadLevelInfo(), which we'll call for each of the level files we loaded. We'll skip the extra lines in each of the files' sections by calling file:read(). Then we'll call the same method with *n as a parameter to read numbers.

Start by opening the file and adding placeholders for actions we'll implement afterward.

LoadingAndSaving/loading.lua
```lua
-- Load a level file and store it in memory
function loadLevelInfo( levelName )
    -- Load the file
    levelName = string.gsub (levelName, "\r", "")
    local fullPath = system.pathForFile( "files/" .. levelName,
        system.ResourceDirectory )
    local fh = io.open( fullPath, "r" )
    -- Skip 3 lines:
    fh:read( "*l" )
    fh:read( "*l" )
    fh:read( "*l" )

    -- Load the map
    -- Load the spawn coordinates
    -- Load the enemy data
end
```

To load the map, first read the map's size. Use these width and height values to loop through each of the rows and columns. When we created the files, we wrote an array that held numbers representing the tile images we wanted to display in each of the map's tiles. Load these into the table that will hold the map for the level.

LoadingAndSaving/loading.lua
```lua
-- Load the map
-- Get the number of map rows and columns
local cols = fh:read( "*n" )
local rows = fh:read( "*n" )
fh:read( "*l" )

-- Read the tiles
tileMap = { }
for i = 1, rows do
    tileMap[i] = { }
    for j = 1, cols do
        -- Read the tile and store it in the tile list
        local tile = fh:read( "*n" )
        tileMap[i][j] = tile
    end
end
```

It's now time for us to read enemy data. Once again, skip the empty lines before reading the number of spawn points. Then, read each spawn point, storing details such as its coordinates and the types of enemies it spawns.

This is also a good time to check that spawn points are in valid locations, just to avoid any mistakes we might make (or that our users might make, if we encourage them to edit levels). For this, include a call to a placeholder function called checkSpawnPoint(). If our game were larger and we developed map-editing tools for it, we could include checks such as these when saving created maps, but for a game this size, doing it in-game is fine.

LoadingAndSaving/loading.lua
```lua
-- Load the spawn coordinates
spawnPoints = { }
spawnPoints[1] = { fh:read( "*n" ), fh:read( "*n" ) }
spawnPoints[2] = { fh:read( "*n" ), fh:read( "*n" ) }
-- Check the spawn points
-- Check the spawn point is valid
if ( ( wrongSpawnPoint( spawnPoints[1], tileMap ) ) or
    ( wrongSpawnPoint( spawnPoints[2], tileMap ) ) ) then
    print "Invalid spawn points"
end
```

The checkSpawnPoint() function is in charge of making sure that spawn points are inside the map area. This ensures that creeps spawned at those locations will be on a tile from the start. To implement the function, compare the map size with the x- and y-coordinates that the function receives.

LoadingAndSaving/loading.lua
```
-- Check whether a spawn point is in the map
function wrongSpawnPoint( coord, tileMap )
    -- Check x and y are within bounds.
    -- Return false if they are not.
    if ( coord[1] < 0 ) or ( coord[1] > #tileMap[1] ) then
        return true
    end
    if ( coord[2] < 0 ) or ( coord[2] > #tileMap ) then
        return true
    end
    return false
end
```

That's it! We've now upgraded our game to include level-definition files for an unlimited number of levels. This is a good time to delete the now-unused level code in levels.lua so that the game is tidy.

10.3 Loading and Saving the Game

Files aren't the only way to store and access information in mobile devices; we can also use SQLite databases, which are more convenient for storing some kinds of game data. SQLite is very intuitive if you're accustomed to SQL, and easy to learn if you're not. Corona's API calls simplify the process of creating and using SQLite databases. We can quickly learn to load and save game data, no matter our current level of database skills.

Adding Stats to the Game

Our game doesn't currently store long-term data about achievements. It's great to master a game, but many players want their accomplishments to be visible for a long time. It would be a pity to play the best game of the week just to see it erased from history when Start Again is tapped. We'll solve this problem by adding a simple stats screen to the game using Corona's SQLite database functions to remember game stats.

Adding a Stats Screen

We need to design our stats screen. We'll keep it simple because saving too many stats can be distracting or even confusing. Let's keep track of games played, enemies killed, gold earned, towers built, and lives lost. These values will be enough to showcase great games, and they'll fit well on most device screens, too.

Begin by creating a storyboard scene called gameover.lua. A new scene avoids object management and the depth-sorting issues we'd encounter by trying to use a new sprite group on the game stage to display stats after a game.

Our new scene's design will be simple: a background image and ten text boxes to hold the stats, as shown in the following figure. Five of the text boxes will be transparent, and will contain the categories measured, such as lives; the five text boxes with backgrounds will show the player's final scores in those categories.

Figure 60—The game-over scene

The background image is called stats_bg.jpg in the chapter's code files, and like in the previous chapter, the image features user-interface elements by Lamoot at OpenGameArt. Display the background as a normal image and add the text boxes as a 2×5 table. For now, display placeholders in the stat boxes using display.newText(), and we'll change these placeholders to display real data later.

The display.newText() function takes a display group, text, x- and y-coordinates, width, height, font, and font size as parameters. Add the values to the stage as text boxes using a table and loop to make things easier. Make sure you add a touch listener to the background image, and you're ready to go.

LoadingAndSaving/gameover.lua
```
-- Prepare the scene
function scene:createScene( event )
    local group = self.view
    -- Add an image to the scene group
```

```
    image = display.newImage("images/game_over.jpg")
    group:insert( image )

    -- Save the stats in the database
    saveStats( )
    loadStats( )
    prepareStatstoDisplay( )

    -- Add the stats boxes
    -- The values are temporary for now
    statNames = { "Games", "Kills", "Gold", "Towers", "Lives Lost" }
    -- statValues = { 1, 2, 3, 4, 5 }
    for i = 1, #statNames do
        -- Display each stat in a box
        local posX = 150
        local posY = 52 + i * 36
        local posX2 = 280
        local txt = display.newText( group, statNames[i], posX,
            posY, 100, 30, native.systemFont, 16 )
        txt:setTextColor( 20, 20, 20 )
        txt = display.newText( group, statValues[i], posX2, posY, 100,
            30, native.systemFont, 16 )
        txt:setTextColor( 255, 240, 230 )
    end
    -- Add the touch listener
    image:addEventListener( "touch", returnToGame )
end
```

Like most of our previous touch listeners, returnToGame() has to call the Corona Storyboard API and tell it to go to the game scene.

```
-- Touch event listener for the menu's background image
-- Goes to the game scene
local returnToGame = function( event )
    -- Only process the event if the player started the tap
    if ( event.phase == "began" ) then
        storyboard.gotoScene( "game" )
    end
end
-- Adds the event listener
function addListener( event )
    bgimage:addEventListener( "touch", gotoGame )
end
```

Now, whenever the game ends, we'll be taken to the stats scene.

Creating a Database

To store the stats, we'll create a new database in the device's documents directory. We'll make sure that the database exists before attempting to load the stats screen, just in case the player has accidentally (or not so accidentally) deleted it. First import the SQLite API, called sqlite3 at the top of the file.

LoadingAndSaving/statslogic.lua
```lua
require( "sqlite3" )
```

To open or create a SQLite database, call sqlite3.open(). Pass the path to the database's filename using system.pathForFile() along with system.DocumentsDirectory to store it in the mobile device's documents directory.

LoadingAndSaving/statslogic.lua
```lua
-- Open or create a new database in a file called "stats.db"
local path = system.pathForFile( "stats.db", system.DocumentsDirectory )
db = sqlite3.open( path )
```

Now we'll add a table to our database to store the stats. Tables are in charge of storing data in databases and can hold several data types. We'll mostly use integers for game statistics, but it's possible to store strings and other kinds of variables, too.

The easiest way to populate or manipulate tables for SQLite is to use an editor like the SQLite Database Browser.[1] SQLite editors offer a spreadsheet-like experience but export to databases or offer a user-friendly way to generate SQL commands that you can then use for SQLite queries like the ones we are about to implement.

Once the database is open, check whether the stats table exists. To check whether a table exists, try to select the table. In Corona, we pass SQL queries using double square brackets (in other words, [[and]]). Use db:exec() to execute a query and db:nrows() to loop through a query's results.

Use a SELECT SQL command to select the stats table, and call db:nrows() to loop through the results. If the query doesn't return a value, we have to create the table and add a row to hold the stat values. Otherwise, we'll proceed to load or save the stats.

LoadingAndSaving/statslogic.lua
```lua
-- Check the table doesn't exist
local exists = false
local query = [[SELECT name FROM sqlite_master WHERE
type='table' AND name='stats']]

for row in db:nrows( query ) do
    tableExists = true
end
```

---

1. The SQLite Database Browser can be found at http://sqlitebrowser.sourceforge.net/.

If the table called stats doesn't exist, create it. Add six columns: one to store a row ID and another one for each of the five values we're storing (games played, enemies killed, gold earned, towers built, and lives lost).

To create a new table, use the CREATE TABLE SQL command. In a table for holding numeric data, create an ID column to sort the numbers, and numeric fields to store numbers. To initialize the stats, add a row of zeros to the table to start, and we'll update the table each time we play the game. Corona requires us to use double square brackets to pass database queries, something that's easy to forget if you're accustomed to other languages.

LoadingAndSaving/statslogic.lua
```lua
-- Create a new table if one doesn't already exist
--    and populate it with empty values
if not tableExists then
    db:exec[[
        CREATE TABLE IF NOT EXISTS stats
            (id INTEGER PRIMARY KEY, games, kills,
            gold, towers, lives);
        INSERT INTO stats VALUES (NULL, 0, 0, 0, 0, 0);
    ]]
end
```

With just five stats to store, we probably didn't need to store them in a database, but doing so gives us room to grow. It will allow us, for example, to save individual stats for each session by adding a date column. This would allow players to monitor their progression over time and might be the sort of feature we'd like to add in later releases or updates.

Keeping Track of Stats

To save gameplay stats, the game will need to keep track of how well the player is playing. Add a Lua table called statistics to game.lua to track player stats. Store stats as named variables in the table to make them easier to access.

LoadingAndSaving/game.lua
```lua
-- Define the stats we'll track
statistics = {
    gamesPlayed = 1,
    kills = 0,
    gold = 0,
    towersBuilt = 0,
    livesLost = 0
}
```

We'll have to update each of the variables we're tracking whenever gameplay affects them. We won't touch the first one, which holds the number of games played since the last game (always 1). To track enemies killed, add 1 to the dead-enemy count each time we remove a dead enemy. In the same function, update the amount of gold earned in this session, because we add some each time the player kills an enemy.

```
statistics.kills = statistics.kills + 1
```

We're also tracking the number of lives the player has lost. Subtract lives when enemies reach the end of the path, so we can update this state in the enemy loop in the game's tick() function. When enemies aren't killed by a tower and we subtract a life, increment the lives-lost stat.

```
statistics.livesLost = statistics.livesLost + 1
```

The last change we need is to update the tower-building function to add 1 to the number of towers built each time we add a tower. This would also be a good spot to add a gold-spent stat if we were tracking one.

```
statistics.towersBuilt = statistics.towersBuilt + 1
```

With stats now being tracked, we'll feed these values into the database to save them.

Saving Stats

To save the stats we've collected, define a SQLite query that uses SQLite's UPDATE function. We have only one row in the database, so there's no need to add the WHERE conditions that might otherwise accompany such SQL queries to tell the database which row to update. To combine variables with a query, close the double square brackets and use the string-concatenation operator (..) to combine the query with a variable.

```
-- Save the stats
function saveStats( )
    -- Create an update query to update the stats table
    local query = [[UPDATE stats SET
        games=games + ]]..statistics.gamesPlayed..[[,
        kills=kills + ]]..statistics.kills..[[,
        gold=gold + ]]..statistics.gold..[[,
        towers=towers + ]]..statistics.towersBuilt..[[,
        lives=lives + ]]..statistics.livesLost..[[;
    ]]
    -- Execute the query
    db:exec( query )
end
```

Now, update the stats row and add the new stats to each column. We're loading the stats screen only at the end of a game, so this code will be called only once per play. Reset the session's stats to 0 after each database update, just in case we run into any application bugs or screen refreshes in the program.

LoadingAndSaving/game.lua
```lua
-- Define the stats we'll track
statistics = {
    gamesPlayed = 1,
    kills = 0,
    gold = 0,
    towersBuilt = 0,
    livesLost = 0
}
```

Now that we're saving the stats in the database, it's time for us to start loading them whenever the player reaches the end-game scene.

Loading Stats

We now have a game that tracks player stats, a database to store them in, and code that does this. The last step is to load the stats in the stats.lua storyboard scene. We've already opened the database to save our stats, so we don't need to open it again. We'll use Corona's database-query functions to load the stats, but instead of calling db:exec() and forgetting about it, we want results returned to us. To get them, use db:nrows(), which enables us to loop through a database query's results.

To load content from the database, we also need the ability to get data from stored tables. In SQL this is called *selecting*, and we use a SELECT to get results. If you're familiar with SQL, it'll make sense that we pass the query as an argument in the form of SELECT * FROM myTable. If you're not familiar with SQL, relying on the aforementioned SQLite editor means you don't need to become familiar with SQL and can just copy and paste the code that you see when you choose rows or columns in the editor.

Use a simple query that selects only one row from the database. We defined an id column in case we ever decide to expand our program to add individual scores to the table, but for now we can simply retrieve rows that have an id equal to 1.

LoadingAndSaving/statslogic.lua
```lua
-- Get the stats from the database
function loadStats( )
    for row in db:nrows("SELECT * FROM stats LIMIT 1") do
        -- Get the row's data
```

```
        statistics.gamesPlayed = row.games
        statistics.kills = row.kills
        statistics.gold = row.gold
        statistics.towersBuilt = row.towers
        statistics.livesLost = row.lives
    end
end
```

Our stats have now been loaded, but we need to display them, so update the placeholder text boxes that we created earlier, setting them to display the values of these variables instead of hard-coded numbers.

LoadingAndSaving/statslogic.lua
```
-- Set the statsValues variable to display it in the stats scene
function prepareStatstoDisplay( )
    statValues = {
        statistics.gamesPlayed,
        statistics.kills,
        statistics.gold,
        statistics.towersBuilt,
        statistics.livesLost
    }
end
```

Our SQLite stats are now loaded and displayed, as shown in the following figure.

Figure 61—Stats

We'll now be able to track how many times the player has started the game or how many enemies have been defeated. This is great, because we'll be able to use those details to improve our game's difficulty when debugging, and it will also let us add achievements in the future.

10.4 Exercises and Expansion Options

Now that we have finished the chapter, here are some ideas you can try to improve this game.

Pausing the Game

The game keeps track of long-term stats and allows us to start a new game after we end a match. However, what can we do if a player wants to stop playing for a moment because of a brief interruption? To allow players to pause the game for a while, we can expand the game to add a pause button. One way to do this is to add a paused variable and then check whether it is active in the tick() function. If the game is paused, the game shouldn't do anything during a given tick.

Stat Enhancements

Right now, the game keeps track of five stats. It would be fun and good practice to add a new type of stat to the game. Try updating the stats panel and SQLite code so that it tracks gold spent by players. Even better, we can enhance our stats display to track top games, allow stats to be reset, or help players evaluate and remember their gameplay in other, more complex ways.

10.5 What We Covered

In this chapter, we saw how to use the Corona file-input and -output functions to store custom level files for our game. We can use these instead of hard-coded arrays to generate game levels, saving us development time and potentially opening the door for user mods. Along the way, we talked about the path functions to access common folders in mobile devices. We also covered how to use Corona with SQLite by coding a stats display for the game. We created a database, added the tables and data, and updated and retrieved stored stats. We also mentioned some common tools that enable non-SQL coders to work with SQLite without having to learn SQL.

Now that players can show their records to their friends and challenge them to get better scores, Tower Defense is a complete game. In the next chapter, we'll start a new game to experiment with accelerometer-based input and advertising tools, and we'll add online support to give international bragging rights to the game's top scorers.

Part V

Physics and Distribution

Having programmed several complete games, we're ready to tackle even more complex mechanics. We'll make a simple ball game where we'll add physics, accelerometer-based input, and high-score systems. After that, we'll cover how to compile and distribute our games in the Android and iOS app stores.

CHAPTER 11

Physics and the Accelerometer

Now that you've learned about pathfinding, we're going to build a new app to experiment with various physics functions.

11.1 What You'll Learn

In this chapter, we'll focus on building upon the physics concepts we've already learned and use them to make a physics-based game. We'll add the following:

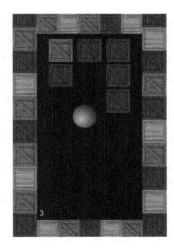

- A ball that will be affected by the laws of physics
- Crates that will disappear when hit by the ball
- Accelerometer-based input

Once we complete this app, players will only have to rotate their phones to play. By the end of the chapter, our app will look like the image shown earlier.

Since we're going to work on a new game, it's a good idea to make sure you remember how to work with sprites and movement. We covered those in the previous chapters, and we'll go through them very quickly in this chapter as we build this game. If you think you've forgotten some of the functions we'll be using, feel free to jump back to Part II, *Planet Defender*, on page 15, at any time.

11.2 Defining the Project

We're going to build a physics-based game where players will have to move their phones to make a ball move. Shaking a phone to move a ball doesn't sound very exciting, so we'll add changing gravity.

So far, we've built both image-based maps and tile-based maps for our games. We didn't add any physics or interactivity to the scenario because we chose how to move the sprites. Yes, we could see the images and tiles, but the units couldn't interact with them. Now we'll use what we already know about physics shapes and extend it to build a physics-based world. In this game, both the ball and the map will have interactive physics shapes attached to them. You guessed it right—this means the ball will collide with the map.

Adding the Sprites

In this game, we'll add a ball sprite and a set of walls that will stop it from moving. We'll keep things simple and add the balls to the borders of the screen, but the process is the same if you want to add walls anywhere else. The ball will be affected by gravity and will move freely across the screen, but we want it to remain within the screen bounds, so the walls will keep it there.

Let's start with the part we already know, which is how to create a sprite. First create a new sprite like we've been doing in all the exercises. Remember to add it to the scene group and to set the frame name you want to display.

```
Physics/game.lua
-- Load the image sheet
gameElements = require( "gamesprites" )
local gameObjectsSheet = graphics.newImageSheet( "images/gamesprites.png",
    gameElements:getSheet() )

-- Make the ball sprite
ball = display.newImage( gameObjectsSheet , gameElements:getFrameIndex( "ball" ))
ball.x = 160
ball.y = 300
group:insert( ball )
```

After that, it's time to add the outer walls. We're using a rectangular game area, so the walls will be around the borders of the screen. It can be tempting to use a single background image for the set of walls, but since we're planning to make them interactive, we'll use four walls. Load the sprites as independent rectangular sprites.

Make sure you add the walls to the scene group. It's easy to run into sprite-removing problems during scene transitions if the sprites aren't in a scene group.

```
Physics/game.lua
-- Make the wall sprites
wallLeft = display.newImage( gameObjectsSheet,
    gameElements:getFrameIndex("wall_left") )
wallTop = display.newImage( gameObjectsSheet,
    gameElements:getFrameIndex( "wall_top") )
wallRight = display.newImage( gameObjectsSheet,
    gameElements:getFrameIndex("wall_right") )
wallBottom = display.newImage( gameObjectsSheet,
    gameElements:getFrameIndex("wall_bottom") )

-- Add them to the group
group:insert( wallLeft )
group:insert( wallTop )
group:insert( wallRight )
group:insert( wallBottom )

-- Set their coordinates
wallLeft:setReferencePoint( display.TopLeftReferencePoint )
wallTop:setReferencePoint( display.TopLeftReferencePoint )
wallRight:setReferencePoint( display.TopLeftReferencePoint )
wallBottom:setReferencePoint( display.TopLeftReferencePoint )
wallRight.x = 270
wallTop.x = 50
wallBottom.x = 50
wallBottom.y = 444
```

If you compile the game now, you'll see the four walls and a ball in the center, as shown in the figure here. We now have to add input to it, because we'll get bored by looking at the screen if it's not interactive.

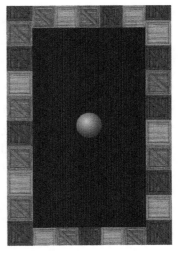

Adding Physics

We know how to use the Corona Physics application programming interface (API) to track for collisions, but we haven't used gravity in any of our previous games. Since we're working on a gravity-based game that features a moving ball, we have to include a gravitational pull. The trick in our game is that we'll change the direction of the gravitational pull depending on the device's accelerometer. That way, players will be able to move their phones as if there were a real ball on them, and it will behave realistically.

Since we've already used physics-based collisions in our games, we can use the same method to add physics shapes to the sprites in the game. You have to build them by either writing the shape coordinates manually or using a tool like PhysicsEditor. Like always, I've used PhysicsEditor for these examples to avoid making mistakes when writing the coordinates. The physics shapes are saved in a file called gameshapes.lua. You can edit it to your liking or generate your own shapes.

After defining the sprite shapes, we have to add them to the sprites on the screen. Right now, the ball on the center of the screen is a static image. Load the physics definitions file and add a physics body to the ball so that it can start moving.

Physics/game.lua
```
-- Load the physics data file
physicsData = (require "gameshapes").physicsData( 1.0 )

-- Attach the circular polygon to the ball
physics.addBody( ball, "ball", physicsData:get( "ball" ) )
```

The borders of the screen need to be walls to make it clear that the ball can't get out of the screen. Otherwise, players might be confused if they don't see anything that stops the ball from falling out of the screen. Since the outside walls are rectangles and we've defined them already, let's add these physics shapes to the sprites.

Physics/game.lua
```
-- Add physics to the walls
physics.addBody( wallLeft, "wall_left", physicsData:get("wall_left") )
physics.addBody( wallTop, "wall_top", physicsData:get("wall_top") )
physics.addBody( wallRight, "wall_right", physicsData:get("wall_right") )
physics.addBody( wallBottom, "wall_bottom", physicsData:get("wall_bottom") )
```

The trick to make the walls static is to define their physics body's bodyType. The default value is "dynamic", which is what we've used before and lets bodies collide with each other and react to gravity. Use "kinematic" to make the body unaffected by gravity, and use "static" to make the bodies stay still. Use "static" for the walls, and we'll use "kinematic" if we want to let players drag an object.

Physics/game.lua
```
wallLeft.bodyType = "static"
wallTop.bodyType = "static"
wallRight.bodyType = "static"
wallBottom.bodyType = "static"
```

That's it! The ball is now static in the center of the screen, like it was before, but the map has a series of physics objects. Feel free to test adding gravity back to check that the physics shapes do collide and behave as intended. If things work as expected, it's time to start listening to accelerometer-based input.

Debugging

Corona's physics engine comes with a very useful system for displaying and debugging physics objects. Instead of using the sprites we're working with, we can draw their polygons or combine both to check that the physics bodies are being attached to the images as expected. To change the visual mode, you can use the setDrawMode() function and pass the style in which you want your physics bodies to be drawn.

```
Physics/game.lua
-- Set the display mode for the physics engine
--   use "hybrid" or "debug" for different results
physics.setDrawMode( "normal" )
```

Aside from "normal", you can also set these parameters:

- debug displays polygons and circles but no sprites. This is good to check for collisions and specific physics problems.

- hybrid shows both sprites and polygons (see the figure here). Use this to check whether you're attaching bodies properly or whether sprites are over- or undersized for their polygons.

- normal is the default draw mode, and it's the one that's typically used for distribution.

Figure 64—Hybrid draw mode

11.3 Adding User Input

In this game, we're not going to use touch-based listeners like we did in the previous games. We'll work with the device's position, so our mouse won't work as an input method. We'll also code a tap-based input system so that we can debug the game easily, and we'll remove it as soon as we don't need to debug.

Instead of transferring our app to our phone each time we want to check whether we've coded our input properly, we can use a tool called Corona

Remote.[1] We'll use a temporary tap-based input system, so it's not necessary to use this tool (but it's good to know it exists).

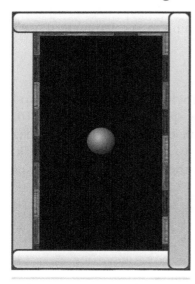

Figure 65—Gravity-changing buttons

We've used buttons in some of our previous projects, and they make debugging much easier. We're going to use four large buttons, one on each border of the screen, and transform them into a virtual accelerometer-like device (see the figure shown here). The device will act as if we had turned it in one direction each time we tap one of the buttons during the simulation. For example, when we tap the right side, the ball will accelerate to the right.

Use the Widget class to make these four new buttons. Make them 30 pixels thick so that they're functional but don't take up too much screen space. Two of them will have a size of 480×30, and the other two will be 30×320. The coordinates have to be based on the borders of the screen. To avoid repeating yourself, use a function to make the button, and add four placeholder functions for the button-tap event.

```
Physics/game.lua
-- Make a new button
function addButton( px, py, w, h, callbackFunc )
    local myButton = widget.newButton{
        id = "btn"..px.."-"..py,
        left = px,
        top = py,
        width = w,
        height = h,
        cornerRadius = 8,
        onEvent = callbackFunc
    }

    -- Make it invisible
    myButton.isVisible = false
    myButton.isHitTestable = true

    return myButton
end
    -- Add 4 buttons to the scene margins
```

---

1. You can find Corona Remote at http://coronaremote.com.

```
group:insert( addButton( 0, 0, 40, 480, gravityLeft ) )
group:insert( addButton( 0, 0, 320, 40, gravityTop ) )
group:insert( addButton( 0, 440, 320, 40, gravityBottom ) )
group:insert( addButton( 280, 0, 40, 480, gravityRight ) )
```

After building the buttons , we have to add some interactivity to them. In this case, since each button simulates turning the device in that direction, the app's gravity will reflect that virtual rotation. That means pushing the right button will add a positive x gravitational acceleration, and pushing the top button will add a negative y acceleration.

Again, Corona comes to the rescue because we have a comfortable physics.set-Gravity() function. We have to pass the x and y accelerations as parameters, and that's about it. In this example, each of the buttons will set an acceleration of 1.0 (about a tenth of that on Earth), but feel free to set any other speed you like. Begin by writing the button functions.

Physics/game.lua
```lua
-- Change the device gravity based on button input
function setButtonGravity( gx, gy )
    physics.setGravity( gx, gy )
end

-- Write the four gravity-related functions
function gravityLeft( event )
    setButtonGravity( -1, 0 )
end
function gravityTop( event )
    setButtonGravity( 0, -1 )
end
function gravityBottom( event )
    setButtonGravity( 0, 1 )
end
function gravityRight( event )
    setButtonGravity( 1, 0 )
end
```

This method is great for debugging if you don't want to transfer your code to your phone each time you compile it. Pressing these buttons is a bit abrupt for a game, though, because gravity changes drastically when they are pressed. A nice alternative is to shift gravity progressively using the real tilt of the mobile device. You guessed it—in the next section we're going to upgrade this to work with the accelerometer.

11.4 Using the Accelerometer

Mobile screens are very small, and using buttons isn't always the best solution. If we don't have to put our hands on the screen, we'll have a lot more space where we'll see the game. That's where the accelerometer appears. I'm sure you've played games where, instead of tapping the screen, you had to tilt the device. That's exactly what we'll do in this game.

Updating Gravity

Even though the accelerometer sounds like a very complicated tool, it's just basic physics. It tracks the device's gravitational pull in each of the three axes, and we can use those numbers to calculate how the device is positioned. If we have a pull only in the x direction, it means the device is completely vertical. If we have a pull in two directions, it means the device is rotated. We'll use the accelerometer to know how the device is positioned. Once we know the rotation, we can move the onscreen objects as if they were being affected by that movement.

The easiest thing we can do is to start using Corona's event listeners. We'll write a new event listener that listens to the accelerometer events. This event has properties like xGravity, yGravity, and zGravity, for each of the gravitational pulls in the phone's three axes. We also have xInstant, yInstant, and zInstant for instant accelerations, which is great to see how fast the phone is being shaken.

We're more interested in long-term or stable accelerations, so let's pick the gravity variables. Write a tilt() method that calls setGravity() to set the gravity depending on the x and y gravitational pulls. Since we started using about one-tenth of the acceleration because of gravity in the previous example, let's continue using that. To do so, multiply the gravity values by 0.1.

Physics/game.lua
```
-- Change gravity based on the phone's tilt
function tilt( event )
    -- Get the x and y accelerations
    local ax = event.xGravity
    local ay = -event.yGravity
    -- Set the gravity based on these values
    physics.setGravity( ax, ay )
end
```

To call the function, add an event listener to Corona's Runtime so that it listens to the accelerometer input and calls the tilt() function you just created. This works just like any other event listener.

Physics/game.lua
```
Runtime:addEventListener( "accelerometer", tilt )
```

You can check whether the tilting code works because we have added a physics shape to the program. You can test the program to check that it doesn't output any errors and it behaves as expected. If you want to be more precise, you can also add a debug line to print desired gravities like the one that's commented out in the code. That helps you see whether the program is handling gravity-related input properly.

Limiting Instant Accelerations

There's a small catch in accelerometer-based input, and that comes when we use instant accelerations and users shake the device very quickly. We'll get large values for each of the accelerations, and the game might stop working properly if we haven't added a maximum value. For example, you might base the speed on the device's instant acceleration, and players who shake the device quickly might move their characters too fast. To avoid that, you can check the vector length and reduce it if necessary. You first calculate the hypotenuse, check its length, and reduce it proportionally if it's too big.

Instead of using gravitational accelerations, we'll now limit instant values in the code we just wrote. Let's update the game so that it limits accelerations to 0.5 meters per second squared. You just have to go back to what you wrote in the tilt() function.

Physics/game.lua
```
-- Limit tilt accelerations
if ( math.abs( ax ) > 0.5 ) then
    ax = math.max( -0.5, math.min( 0.5, ax ) )
end
if ( math.abs( ay ) > 0.5 ) then
    ay = math.max( -0.5, math.min( 0.5, ay ) )
end
```

Now you can check whether the game gets the device's position properly or whether you've triggered any errors. Since you're printing the accelerometer details to the console, it's easy to spot mistakes. You can pick instant or gravitational accelerations depending on the type of game you want to make. If you don't like the way the program behaves, you can change the acceleration values you've used in the physics simulation and either increase or decrease them to your liking.

11.5 Working with Removable Crates

At this point, the app works using physics, but it's boring to look at if we don't have any goals. Let's add a few crates so that the ball can collide against them. If the ball hits them, we'll remove them from the stage. Since we're using Corona's Physics API, collisions will take place automatically, and we'll only have to add physics bodies and a function that should react to collisions.

Adding Crates

The chapter's code files come with three crate images called crate1, crate2, and crate3. Each of them is 50×50 pixels in size. Since we don't have much screen space left, we can add three rows by three columns of crates.

To do this, perform two loops to add three rows and three columns of equidistant crates, and add a physics body to their images. The image sheet's details are included in the gamesprites.lua file, and the physics bodies are in gameshapes.lua. As always, they have been generated using TexturePacker and PhysicsEditor, respectively, but you can code them manually or using any other equivalent program.

Since we're going to remove crates that have been hit by the ball, add an isAlive property and another one called type to store the object's type: a crate variable. As always, add them to the group and a crates table to make it easier to manage them.

```
Physics/game.lua
-- Add the crates
for i = 0, 2 do
    for j = 0, 2 do
        -- Add a crate
        local crateName = "crate" .. math.random( 3 )
        local crate = display.newImage( gameObjectsSheet,
            gameElements:getFrameIndex( crateName ) )
        crate.x = 100 + 60 * j
        crate.y = 80 + 55 * i

        -- Define its properties
        crate.type = TYPE_CRATE
        crate.isAlive = true
        -- Add it to the group and table
        group:insert( crate )
        crates[ #crates + 1 ] = crate
        -- Add crate bodies
        physics.addBody( crate, "crate", physicsData:get( crateName ) )
        crate.bodyType = "kinematic"
    end
end
```

With this code, we'll be able to check the type property before removing an object when the ball collides with something.

Listening to Collisions

Adding physics objects without checking their collisions won't work with the crates, so let's add a collision listener to the ball. To do so, set its collision property to a placeholder function called ballCollision(), and add a collision event listener to the ball. Whenever it collides against something, it will trigger the ballCollision() function.

```
Physics/game.lua
-- Add the collision listener
ball.collision = ballCollision
ball:addEventListener( "collision", ball )
```

The next step is to write a function that will be triggered whenever the ball collides with another physics body. The function has to check the type property of the object that has collided with the ball. Since we've set it to equal a variable called TILE_CRATE in crate variables, set its isAlive variable to false.

```
Physics/game.lua
-- Collision listener function
function ballCollision( self, event )
    if ( event.phase == "began" ) then
        local object = event.other

        -- Remove active crates
        if ( ( object.type == TYPE_CRATE ) and
            ( object.isAlive == true ) )then
            object.isAlive = false
```

After making these changes, we'll use the isAlive variable to remove inactive crates.

Removing Inactive Crates

The most intuitive way to remove inactive crates would be within the collision function, but removing objects in the middle of a Box2D collision can sometimes lead to problems. To avoid this, we'll remove inactive crates from the tick() function in the game. As always, add an enterFrame event listener to the scene-creation function.

```
Physics/game.lua
-- Tick
Runtime:addEventListener( "enterFrame", tick )
```

Within the tick function, the only task we have to do is to loop through the crates and remove those that are inactive. Loop backward to avoid skipping crates during the loop, and call removeSelf() to remove a crate. Remember that we haven't coded any class-specific removeMe() functions for crates, so we have to use the default Corona functions.

Physics/game.lua
```
-- Tick function
function tick( event )
    -- Remove inactive crates
    for i = #crates, 1, -1 do
        if ( crates[i].isAlive == false ) then
            crates[i]:removeSelf( )
            removeTableRows( crates, i )
        end
    end
end
```

If you compile the program at this stage, the crates will appear on the stage, and you'll be able to destroy them as soon as the ball collides with them.

Adding Scores

Breaking crates is nice, but it can be more fun to keep track of the player's score. Whenever the ball breaks a crate, we'll increase the score. Start by declaring scoreTxt and score variables to hold the score text box and score, respectively.

Physics/game.lua
```
-- Score variables
local score = 0
local scoreTxt
```

When the game starts, add a text box to the stage that holds the player's score. To do so, use display.newText() like we did in the previous chapter. You can place it in the bottom-left area of the screen (at coordinates 55, 420) and make it 100×20 pixels in size.

Physics/game.lua
```
-- Show the score
scoreTxt = display.newText( group, score, 55,
    420, 100, 20, native.systemFont, 16 )
```

Now update the collision function so that it adds one point to the score and updates the score text field. You can update a text field's content by changing its text property.

Physics/game.lua
```
-- Collision listener function
function ballCollision( self, event )
    if ( event.phase == "began" ) then
        local object = event.other
```

```
        -- Remove active crates
        if ( ( object.type == TYPE_CRATE ) and
            ( object.isAlive == true ) )then
            object.isAlive = false
            -- Update the score
            score = score + 1
            scoreTxt.text = score
        end
    end
end
```

This basic Breakout-style game is finally done, and we even have a score-tracking system. You can compile the game at this stage and check that the score is updating properly.

11.6 Exercises and Expansion Options

Now that we have finished the chapter, here are some ideas you can try to improve this game.

Adding Bonuses

Some players are more skilled than others, so they might get bored if they can't do anything useful in the game. Try to add a variable to track the score, and a few power-ups at random accessible locations on the maps. If players get the bonus on time, then the bonus sprite disappears, and bonus points are added to the total score.

Adding Obstacles

Some games have really cool physics-based obstacle tracks. Instead of designing a map with borders where the players just have to move the ball around, try adding a few obstacles. If you want even more fun, you can make deadly obstacles. For example, draw some spikes and make the ball die if it hits them. You can also add some shapes that disappear when the ball collides against them and either add or subtract points. If you're feeling creative, you can make some of the spikes interactive using physics, which would create an even more challenging game.

11.7 What We Covered

In this chapter, we built a simple but fun game that we've used to practice how to add physics-based behaviors and accelerometer-based input. A ball moves around the screen and collides with obstacles, and players have to move their phones to move the ball. We've been able to code all this very quickly using Corona's default API calls. Since we have also coded a button-based input, we don't have to test the game using a mobile device—we can use the mouse and emulator to test the program and just check that everything functions when we work on input-specific issues. With what we've learned, we can let a player shake the phone to simulate an earthquake or to tilt a ship according to the phone's position to see how dozens of little sailors get dizzy. The possibilities are endless.

Now that we've built so many games, it's time to learn how to share them with the world. In the next chapter, we'll focus on publishing this app and adding monetization options. After all, if we code games but store them on a hard drive, we'll never know if others like them.

CHAPTER 12

Publishing Our Apps

We've built several games, and it's time for us to share them with the world!

12.1 What You'll Learn

In this chapter, we'll do the following:

- See how to upload games to four app markets to make our games accessible from iPhones, Nooks, Kindles, and Android phones

- Add advertisements and in-app purchases

We'll focus on applying these changes to the game we made in the previous chapter, but feel free to use a different game while you work through the chapter's content.

12.2 Building and Publishing Our Apps

Publishing a game is one of the most exciting moments in game development. It's also a bit stressful and full of "what ifs": What if there are bugs? What if nobody likes it? It's normal to be a bit scared when you launch your game, but you can reduce those fears by testing it before its launch and making sure that it's as good as you want it to be.

Once we've gathered enough courage to start distributing the game, the publishing process is really easy. You have to follow different steps depending on whether you want to release it for Android or iOS, but both paths are quite simple to follow. It's best to release your games for both platforms, because Corona does most of the work for you. You can increase your user base just by making your app available for both iOS and Android devices.

Adding Icons

Apps without icons won't sell easily in the app stores because users won't be able to know what the game looks like or what it's about, so let's add an icon to our game. To do this, we need eight images in total: four for Android and four for iOS, as shown in the following table. These requirements change whenever screen resolutions improve, so it's always good to check the latest specifications for iOS and Android.[1,2]

Icon Size	File Name	Device Type
96×96	Icon-xhdpi.png	Extra-high-density Android
72×72	Icon-hdpi.png	High-density Android
48×48	Icon-mdpi.png	Medium-res Android
36×36	Icon-ldpi.png	Low-res Android
144×144	Icon@2x.png	Retina iPhone and iPod touch
114×114	Icon@2x.png	Retina iPhone and iPod touch
72×72	Icon-72.png	iPad
57×57	Icon.png	Other iOS devices

The Android building process takes care of automatically adding the icons to your app, so you only have to make sure to add the files to the folder. To add the files to your iOS projects, you must also update the build.settings file and store variables called CFBundleIconFiles and CFBundleIconFile to set the icon names.

```
PublishGame/build.settings
settings = {
    iphone = {
        plist = {
            -- Application icons
            CFBundleIconFile = "Icon.png",
            CFBundleIconFiles = {
                "Icon.png",
                "Icon@2x.png",
                "Icon-72.png",
            },
        }
    },
}
```

---

1. Get the list of required sizes for the iOS App Store from http://developer.apple.com/library/ios/ #documentation/userexperience/conceptual/mobilehig/IconsImages/IconsImages.html.

2. Get information about icon sizes required for the Google Play store here: http://developer.android.com/design/style/iconography.html.

Once you've done this, you'll also need 512×512 and 1024×1024 icons for the Android and iOS app stores, respectively. You won't need those in your project folder, but it's easier to make them now and keep them around until you're submitting the app to the app stores.

Multiple-Resolution Support

There are hundreds of mobile-phone models, with various screen sizes and resolutions. That's great for users because they can see apps adapted to their screens. For us developers, that means a bit more work. Up to this point, we've used a resolution of 320×480, like some of the early iPhones had. Luckily, Corona lets us use letterbox scaling (in other words, not distorting image proportions) for our apps and is also compatible with using high-res images for tablet and Retina iOS devices.

Using Letterbox Scaling

To use letterbox scaling, we'll continue defining our app sizes as 320×480, but we'll use a larger background so that devices don't show black margins around the app. Corona recommends using image sizes of 380×570, so we'll use that proportion for the background. Since these images are bigger than 512 pixels, you'll have to tell Corona to bypass the safety maximum-image-size limit on iPhones. That means passing an optional Boolean parameter as true whenever you call display.newImage().

For foreground images, this means that the visible area for our games can range from (-30, -45) to (350, 525), or the other way around if you're using a landscape orientation. The playable area should still be 320×480 so that everyone can interact with units, but we have to add and remove units and objects outside the larger area so players don't see them appear from nowhere.

Loading Higher-Resolution Images

Some recent phones and tablets have much better screens than older ones. It's a pity that users with those newer phones can't see better graphics, so we have an option to load different images depending on the device's resolution. You can do that using the imageSuffix property in your game's config.lua.

If you use this property, you can set a coefficient to tell Corona when to load the different image sizes. For example, if you want to load a different image set when users have a screen that is 150 percent larger than the default size you're using (in this case, 320), the coefficient will be 1.5. If it's twice the size, then the coefficient will be 2. You can use both 1.5 and 2 to use a total of three image sets, like this:

PublishingAndAds/config.lua
```lua
application = {
    content = {
        imageSuffix = {
            ["-m"] = 1.5,
            ["-l"] = 2,
        }
    },
}
```

In the previous code, your images would use the normal names for normal (1.0) resolutions, such as imageName.png. Images scaled by a coefficient of 1.5 would use the -m suffix, and you'd call them imageName-m.png. The largest images would be called imageName-l.png. You can change these suffixes to anything you like.

The problem with this solution is that this makes you create three sets of images for your game. It's easier to use only two sets. Corona recommends using a factor of 1.8 if you use only two sets of images so that all tablets access the larger images. To do that, you'd have to write only one suffix.

PublishingAndAds/config.lua
```lua
application = {
    content = {
        imageSuffix = {
            ["-med"] = 1.8,
        }
    },
}
```

You can play around with these settings and adapt them to your games. Just remember that whenever you add a new texture coefficient, you're also multiplying the number of images you're shipping with your game, so players will take longer to download it.

Building iOS Apps

Corona lets you build for iOS if you have a Mac. You also need to have Xcode installed, but you can get it easily from the Mac App Store. This is bad news for any Windows users, but I'm sure you can collaborate with a friend or relative with a Mac if you want to release your games in the App Store. You can also use cloud-based Mac rental services like XCodeClub,[3] where you can rent a virtual Mac for a few days while you build your apps.

---

3. XCodeClub can be found at http://www.xcodeclub.com.

The first step to publish your app for iOS is to get an iOS developer account. To do so, you have to sign up for the iOS developer program through the Apple website.[4] You'll have to pay a fee (which was $99 yearly at the time this book was published) and provide some of your personal details.

If you already have an iOS developer account, then you don't need to create a new one. If you don't, then don't worry. This step won't take long, and the sign-up system is user-friendly.

Once you have an iOS developer account, the next step is to get a certificate to test your apps in the simulator. You'll get this using the iPhone Dev Portal if you're an active iPhone developer using Mac OS.

Getting a Certificate-Signing Request

Mac OS makes it really easy to get a certificate-signing request (CSR). You have to go to your Utilities folder and find the Keychain Access program. In that program, click the menu (Keychain Access), and select "Request a certificate from a Certificate Authority" from the Certificate Assistant subheader.

This will open a new window with the Certificate Assistant. You'll be prompted to enter your email address and a common name. For the email address, use the one you used to sign up as an Apple developer. For the common name, you can use your team name or your own name. Make sure you choose to save the certificate-signing request to disk and that you want to define the key-pair information.

The Apple Dev Portal works with RSA keys and 2048-bit key sizes. Choose those options on the next screen, and you're ready to go!

Uploading the CSR to Apple

Visit the iPhone Dev Portal and go to the Certificates section. In that section, select the option to add a new certificate and choose the CSR file you just created.

Download your signed development certificate and run the file. You will get a message allowing you to add the developer certificate to your Keychain. That's it! You're now able to build apps for iOS.

Getting an App ID

An App ID is basically a string of characters that helps identify the app, and all apps need an App ID before they can be deployed. Sometimes you won't

---

4.   The iOS developer program's website can be found at http://developer.apple.com/iphone/program/.

need to use it frequently, but you might have to if you ever decide to access external hardware or send push notifications. To create a new App ID, go to the iPhone Dev Portal, and click App IDs.

If you've coded in Java, you'll remember that project naming usually follows the reverse domain notation. If your website is myawesomewebsite.com, then you used com.myawesomewebsite.projectname for your project. Here, we'll do the same for App IDs, although Apple adds a unique prefix to each app, so your final App ID might be ABCDEFGHIJ.com.myawesomewebsite.project-name.

After submitting the App ID form, you'll be able to use this new App ID with your new app. We'll use it when creating provisioning profiles.

Adding iOS Devices

Among other features, the iPhone Dev Portal lets you add devices to run and test your programs. To register a device, you can use iTunes to get its unique device identification (UDID) and input that into the iPhone Developers website.

Connect the device to your computer, open iTunes, and view the summary page. There, you'll see some of its technical details, but the UDID is nowhere to be seen! To show it, you have to click the serial number, and it will magically transform into your UDID. Make sure you copy it for the next step.

Back in the iPhone Dev Portal, you can go to the "devices" page and select the option to add a new device. There you'll have to write a name and the device's ID. Use a name you can recognize (for example, Jane's iPhone) and enter the UDID you just copied.

Defining Provisioning Profiles

When you build an app, you have to set a series of preferences. To make our life simpler, iOS works with something called *provisioning profiles*. The profiles save these settings so that we can define them once and use them over and over. We'll usually work with two profiles: Ad Hoc and Distribution. The former is for testing, and the latter is what we'll use to export our app.

You can make a new provisioning profile in the iPhone Dev Portal. Visit the Provisioning page and select the Distribution tab. It can be intuitive to use Development because we're developing an app, but Corona doesn't work with that type of provisioning profile.

Create a new profile and set its distribution method (to Ad Hoc if you're testing and to Distribution if you're launching an app), set a name for it, and select your game's App ID.

Once you've created the profile, you can download it to your Provisioning Profiles folder,[5] and you'll be able to use it during development.

Building Your iOS App

Corona makes building really simple, and it's similar to the way in which we open an app to run it in the simulator. We only have to open the simulator and select Open for Build for whatever project we want to build.

The Build menu will give you a series of options, such as the application name you want to set, its version, and the destination folder. You'll also have to choose the development certificate you created before.

Installing Ad Hoc apps: If your phone is connected to iTunes, you can run the application you just built by dragging it to iTunes. Your phone will sync, and you'll soon be able to play your game.

Submitting Distribution apps: Go to the iPhone Dev Center, and go to the iTunes Connect page. You'll have to agree to Apple's contracts, and you'll be able to choose your pricing and submit your app. Make sure you have the following ready:

- A 1024×1024 .png icon for your application

- At least one screenshot

- At least one launch image that will be displayed while the app is loading[6]

- A .zip file containing the application

After you've submitted the app, it will enter the review stage. Breathe deeply and relax—you've sent it! Don't hold your breath until you receive an answer, though, because it can take several weeks for an app to be approved.

Building Android Apps

Just like for iOS apps, you need to sign your Android applications. However, you don't need to get them signed by anyone else; you can self-sign them. To do this, you can use a program like Keytool, which is recommended on the Android website, or you can go with your Mac Keychain on the Mac OS or with OpenSSL on Windows.[7]

---

5. Your Provisioning Profiles folder can be found at /Users/[username]/Library/MobileDevice/Provisioning Profiles.
6. Get the list of required launch-image sizes for the iOS app store from http://developer.apple.com/library/ios/#documentation/userexperience/conceptual/mobilehig/IconsImages/IconsImages.html.
7. Download OpenSSL from http://www.openssl.org.

Regardless of the program you use, the key needs to have a size of 2048. You should also set a long validity. The Android Developers' website recommends using at least 10,000 days, but choose any value you like. You'll set these visually if you use the Keychain utility in Mac. On Windows, the command for OpenSSL is also straightforward. Use the openssl req method in the console.

PublishingAndAds/openssl.txt
```
openssl req -new -newkey rsa:2048 -out csr.csr ^
-subj "/emailAddress=email@yoursite.com, CN=Team Leader Name"
```

Once you have a signed certificate, you can choose the Open for Build option in the Corona simulator. You will get a panel where you'll have to write the application name, its version, a Java-like package name, and the certificate you'll use to sign it (Figure 66, *Build an Android app*, on page 205). The package name sounds a bit confusing, but just use the same system you used for the iOS key: write something like com.myawesomewebsite.projectname if your domain name is myawesomewebsite.com.

That's it! To install your app, you'll have to either use the commands from the Android SDK (if you have installed it) or download it directly to your phone. If you want to connect your phone to your computer and use the Android SDK, you will have to use the adb install command to install the app. If you're reinstalling an app, you'll first have to use the adb uninstall command to remove it.

PublishingAndAds/installing.txt
```
-- First, uninstall the app
--   Use reverse domain notation
adb uninstall com.mydomain.gamename

-- Now install it again
--   Use the apk name
adb install PublishGame.apk
```

Depending on the target platform you chose in the menu, you can upload your app to the Google Play, Kindle Fire, and Nook Color stores. Make sure you have promotional icons, thumbnails, screenshots, and promotional images for your apps, and the submission process is really simple.

12.3 Testing on Our Phones

Once we're happy with how we've coded our apps, it's time for us to test them on our own phones. This is really important because some errors don't appear in the Corona simulator, and you have to check whether the app works when using a real device. The easiest way to be rejected from an app store is if your app crashes in the main menu, so let's see how to avoid this by using

Figure 66—Build an Android app.

debugging tools on our phones. If you don't have an Android or iOS device and you want to make games for those platforms, try to get some friends to lend you their devices for a while—invite them over for some pizza, and you can debug.

Debugging on iOS

If you've followed the previous steps to get an Ad Hoc provisioning profile, you can build your app using that option. If you want to use iTunes (which is considerably easier than other options), open it up and drag the file to the library. You can sync the file to your device normally.

You can also transfer your apps to a phone using Xcode or the iPhone configuration utility.[8] Both programs are really intuitive, and you don't need to have the device linked to your iTunes account to use them. This is great to install your apps on your friends' phones so that they carry them around and do some free advertising for you.

---

8. Download the iPhone Configuration Utility from http://www.apple.com/uk/support/iphone/enterprise/.

Debugging on Android

The first step to debug on an Android device is to download the Android ADB tools, which you can get as part of the Android SDK.[9] Download the bundle and remember where you've unpacked it, because you'll use it whenever you want to debug an Android program on your phone.

Once you've downloaded the Android SDK, you'll have to be able to connect your phone to your PC to transfer everything there. To do that, you may need the Android OEM USB drivers, depending on your OS.[10] As well as that, you might need a program to install .apk files on your phone. There are dozens of free options in the Google Play store, so take your pick. You can also use the adb tools (adb install) to install the file. Finally, you'll have to go to your phone's settings and enable the debugging option so that you get messages on your computer.

Now that both your computer and your phone are ready to debug your apps, go to the platform-tools folder in the Android sdk folder, and run adb.exe from the command window. You can run it using many different filtering options,[11] but my favorite is to use a filter for Corona. The following code prints anything related to your Corona apps (including print() commands) and ignores everything else:

PublishingAndAds/debugging.txt
```
adb logcat Corona:V *:S
```

Once you get this working, you're good to go. Sometimes debugging using the traditional debug program on Android isn't enough, though. The app may crash, and the debugger might not give you any reasons. To solve this, you can use the print() function to narrow down the problem and try to fix it. Commenting sections of code might not be a neat solution in most cases, but it can work if the debugging tool isn't doing the job.

12.4 Selling In-App Features

If you've used a modern smartphone or tablet, I'm sure you've seen dozens of apps with in-app purchases. These apps let players unlock extra content or buy upgrades for their iOS and Android games. These unlock features are

---

9. Download the Android software development kit (SDK) from http://developer.android.com/sdk/index.html.
10. Learn how to install the Android OEM USB drivers in http://developer.android.com/tools/extras/oem-usb.html.
11. Check the list of Android debugging options here: http://developer.android.com/tools/debugging/debugging-log.html.

usually optional and let users choose if they want to play the base game or buy some of those bonuses to improve their characters or get extra maps. It's a great solution if you want to let your players enjoy the game before paying or if you want to distribute part of the game as an optional purchase.

If you're going to use Android for your apps, the first step is to update the build.settings file to give billing permission to the Android app. This consists of adding or updating a variable called usesPermissions so that it includes the billing module (com.android.vending.BILLING).

PublishGame/build.settings
```
settings = {
    -- Add Android billing permissions
    android =
    {
        usesPermissions =
        {
            "com.android.vending.BILLING",
        }
    }
}
```

If you want to work with both application stores at once (iOS and Android), then you need to import different libraries. Corona comes with a variable called store.availableStores that lets us know whether the Google or Apple stores are available. We'll process each store independently, because the product IDs are different for both platforms.

Corona comes with a store library that contains all of the functions you'll need to sell items via the app. You'll load the library, initialize it, and then get the product list to tempt users to buy the products. The first step is to require the library and initialize it using init() after the program starts running. Note that there are two init() functions, depending on which app store is available. I'm going to add a placeholder callback function to each of the init() functions that will be called after users purchase. We don't have to worry about that function yet.

PublishGame/purchasing.lua
```
-- Store permissions
if store.availableStores.apple then
    store.init("apple", transactionCallback)
elseif store.availableStores.google then
    store.init("google", transactionCallback)
end
```

Now we need to store the items we'll be working with. We'll define these in their corresponding portals. For iPhone, visit the iPhone Dev Center and get item IDs for everything you want to sell. If you are using Android, the Google Play developer console will let you define them.

You can't get the list of available items in Corona, so you have to hard-code the item IDs. Once you have them, store them in a list in your app. Store the item IDs for iOS as a list of strings. Android needs a table with an item name (title), description, item ID (productIdentifier), and price for each item. Android comes with a set of testing product IDs during the development stages so that you can check what happens when transactions work or fail, so feel free to use them during development rather than the real item IDs you'll sell.

PublishGame/purchasing.lua

```
-- The list of products for iOS devices
local productListIOS =
{
    "com.createMobileGamesWithCorona.MyGame.BackgroundImage",
}

-- The product list for google store items
--    Note: these are the reserved item IDs for testing purchases

local googleProductList =
{
    {
        title = "Background Image",
        description = "A shiny background image",
        productIdentifier = "android.test.purchased",
        price = 0.99

        -- use android.test.canceled or
        --    android.test.item_unavailable for alternate testing results
    }
}
```

After that, we'll add a new button to the main menu for each item we have. We don't know if we'll want to sell the items forever, so we always want to check with the server first. To get the product list, use the loadProducts() function in iOS. The function receives a second parameter, which is the name of the function that will be called after the product information is received (e.g., productsLoaded()). Android can't get the product details externally, so call a placeholder function named showProductSaleImages(), and we'll show items manually.

PublishGame/purchasing.lua

```
-- Show the products using button widgets
function showProductSaleImages( )
    for i = 1, #productsList do
        local myButton = widget.newButton{
            id = "btn"..i,
            left = 75,
            top = 450 - 50 * i,
```

```
                label = "Buy "..productsList[i].price,
                width = 170, height = 40,
                cornerRadius = 8,
                onEvent = purchaseBG
            }
        buyButtons:insert( myButton )
    end
end


-- Load the product information and display it
if store.canLoadProducts then
    -- iOS: load the product list (online)
    currentStore = "apple"
    productsList = productListIOS
    store.loadProducts( productListIOS, productsLoaded )
else
    -- Android: Add the data manually
    currentStore = "android"
    productsList = googleProductList
    showProductSaleImages( )
end
```

Since we haven't written the productsLoaded() function yet, it's a good time to do so. This function is a callback, so we'll get what the loadProducts() function passes us: a table called products and a list called invalidProducts, which is a list of the IDs that we passed but that didn't exist.

The table of products has a title, price, description, and productIdentifier, just like those we hard-coded for the Android market. That's great, because we can pass them to the showProductSaleImages() function and write the code for both stores at the same time.

The only item that exists is a $0.99 background-image unlock. We don't know if we'll at some point want to change the price, so don't hard-code it. Instead, use the price variable to show how much it costs. The rest is just adding a normal button and a function call, such as purchaseBG(), in case users want to buy the item.

PublishGame/purchasing.lua

```
-- Set the loaded products on iOS
function productsLoaded( event )
    -- Store the product list
    productsList = event.products

    -- Call the display image
    showProductSaleImages( )
end
```

Users can now see that we're selling a background! If they click the unlock button, they'll trigger the purchaseBG() function. We're working with the same product ID as before, so we can pass it to Corona's purchase() function as a list. Corona will call the function callback we set in the init() function once the request is sent.

PublishGame/purchasing.lua
```lua
-- Purchase an item from the product list
function purchaseBG( event )
    if ( event.phase == "ended" ) then
        store.purchase( { productsList[1].productIdentifier } )
    end
end
```

In the transactionCallback() function, we'll receive a series of details about how the transaction went. We'll basically have to check its state. If it's equal to either purchased or restored, then the item has been bought, and we can display a different background image. Make sure you call finishTransaction() after you process the transaction so that the App Store doesn't keep sending you transaction information each time that the app is loaded.

PublishGame/purchasing.lua
```lua
-- Handle app transactions
function transactionCallback( event )
    if event.transaction.state == "purchased" then
        -- Success!
        backgroundUnlocked = 1
        print( "the user bought the background" )
        backgroundImg.isVisible = true
        buyButtons.isVisible = false
    end

    store.finishTransaction( event.transaction )
end
```

The last step is to load a different background image by checking whether fullGameVersion is equal to 1.

Now that we know how to add purchasing features to our apps, we can lower the base cost and let players choose how much they want to spend in our games. We'll be able to keep updating our apps free of cost for some users and add optional paid downloadable content (DLC) for those who want to pay for a more complex game. As always, make sure you price your app coherently; nobody will buy DLC if it's priced way above the cost of a new app.

12.5 Adding Advertisements

Sometimes apps are too simple to sell, or we might want to give them away for free to get a broader user base. Since we don't get money from the app stores if our apps are free, we have to use a different method to generate income. Ads are a great solution: we show them when the game or one of the levels loads, and we get a small amount of money from them. That way, players can play for free, and we can still make money.

To incorporate ads in Corona, we have to include the ads library, initialize the ads, and show them whenever we want. Corona comes with a really useful library that does most of the work for us. If we use one of the advertising companies that come bundled with Corona (such as Inneractive or InMobi[12,13]), we need to write only three lines of code to show ads.

First include the library in the code file where you're going to work with ads. If you want to show them before the menu loads, go to the menu scene. Since we're working with only one scene in this game, use the game.lua scene. Include the library by requiring the ads file, and then initialize the InMobi library using the init() function with the library name and your App ID.

PublishGame/advertising.lua
```
-- Load the ads library

local ads = require "ads"
ADS_APP_ID = nil -- This should be your ads app ID
```

Now call the show() function to display the ad whenever you want. In this case, a great time to show it is when the game starts. The show() function takes the ad type as the first parameter, and an optional list of parameters afterward. This list includes the x- and y-coordinates, the interval of seconds between ads, and testMode to indicate that you are testing the ads. You'll set testMode to false once you launch your app.

PublishGame/advertising.lua
```
-- Store the settings for the game's ads
AD_NETWORK = "inmobi"
-- Init the ads API
ads.init( AD_NETWORK, ADS_APP_ID )
-- Show an inMobi ad
function showInMobiAds( )
    ads.show( "banner300x250", { x=0, y=0, interval=60, testMode=true } )
    -- Remember to set testMode = false when you build your app!
end
```

---

12. Inneractive: http://www.inner-active.com/
13. InMobi: http://www.inmobi.com/url/registration-form/

If you want to load Inneractive ads instead of using inMobi, you can use the same functions. Just change the init() function so that it calls Inneractive instead of InMobi. This network also lets you specify a third parameter in the function, which is a function listener to be called when an ad is displayed. Update the code, and add a small callback to count the number of ads displayed. This callback is great if you want to check how users behave and how ads are distributed among them.

PublishGame/advertising.lua
```lua
AD_NETWORK = "inneractive"

-- Show inneractive ads
function showInneractiveAds( )
    ads.show( "fullscreen", { x=adX, y=adY, interval=60,
        testMode=true }, inneractiveListener )
    -- Remember to set testMode = false when you build your app!
end
```

That's it! Corona ads are this easy. You might not like the ad size we've used in this example, but you can also change that. Both ad networks come with several ad sizes that you can change depending on your application type and your preferences.

Great! Now you can include ads in any game as an alternative income source. It's important not to overuse them, though. Players will accept a few ads now and then, but seeing an ad every five seconds can destroy the fun of the game. And remember, if players stop playing, the ads will stop showing. It's best to reach a balance between ads and game time.

12.6 Exercise: Modifying the Game

Now that we've finished the chapter, let's take a look at a set of changes we can make to improve this game.

Blocking Ads with In-App Purchases

It's great to make money from ads, but some players find it annoying. It's difficult to choose whether to make a game free and earn less or to sell it and get fewer players. The hybrid solution is to provide the game for free (with ads) and sell an in-app upgrade so that ads aren't shown for paying users. Before showing an ad, check whether the user has bought the ad-free upgrade and show the ad only if not.

12.7 What We Covered

This chapter has been really intense, and we covered how to take our games from completion to glory. We can now publish games in the Apple App Store, in the Android Market, and for Nook Color and Kindle Fire devices. We also discussed how to sell in-game content through in-app purchases so that we can add optional upgrades for our players. If we'd rather not charge users, we can instead show ads during loading screens or before the end of a level.

We've covered many topics and learned how to code fun games. Try adding new elements to make the games more challenging, and check back in on the book forum pages at http://forums.pragprog.com/forums/247 and share what you are working on.

Good luck, and don't forget to enjoy making your games!

Corona Resources

When making games, we have to juggle various development areas: coding, art, and game design. It can be complicated to combine all these if we're working in a small team, and development time frames can be really long unless we use premade assets and other productivity tools.

A1.1 Corona Development Tools

The Corona simulator lets you create your games by typing code in text editors, but sometimes it's much faster to use third-party tools to automate some of the actions. We can use sprite-management tools, physics editors, and even tile and map editors and libraries.

PhysicsEditor

PhysicsEditor is a program that lets you create physics shapes for your games using only your mouse. You need to drag a sprite to the program, and the program will detect its borders and generate a collision area. You can also change these collision areas to your tastes so that the physics bodies in your games behave in exactly the way you want them to. It works on both Windows and Mac OS.

http://www.codeandweb.com/physicseditor

TexturePacker

TexturePacker automates one of the most annoying tasks for a Corona game developer: storing lists of images to create sprites and merging all sprites in image sheets to reduce the number of resources that need to be loaded. This program outputs Corona-friendly sprite files to simplify sprite creation. It works on both Windows and Mac OS.

http://www.codeandweb.com/texturepacker/coronasdk

Corona Remote

Corona Remote is an app for your iPhone that lets you transmit its accelerometer-based movement to your computer. This is great because you can use it to debug your accelerometer-based apps from the simulator without having to transfer them to a phone.

http://www.coronaremote.com/

Lime

This is a great library to make 2D tile-based games. It's open source under the MIT license and comes with a lot of features that you can use right out of the box: layers, tile properties, map scrolling, parallax, and physics. You can make your maps using Tiled, a graphical interface, and use them in Corona. Since it's a library for Corona, you can use it on both Windows and Mac.

http://lime.outlawgametools.com/

A1.2 Corona Development Environments

Outlaw

One of the greatest disadvantages of using a text editor in Corona is that it doesn't autocomplete your text, and you have to write each function complete-ly. Outlaw is a development environment where you can easily access your project's assets and write code. Best of all, it comes with autocomplete so that you can save many keystrokes when you code your games. It works on both Windows and Mac OS, and it has a free Lite version.

http://outlawgametools.com/

Krea IDE

If you don't like to type sprite-related code in Corona, consider the Krea integrated development environment (IDE), which lets you edit the stage graphically. It makes things more intuitive and visual during development so that you don't need to recompile the program to see the changes each time you change a sprite's location. It works on Windows only.

https://www.native-software.com

Level Director

Level Director lets you edit your levels graphically, and it does most of the work of loading assets, tracing collision polygons, drawing joints between physics shapes, handling parallax scrolling, and much more. It's compatible with both TexturePacker and PhysicsEditor, and it works on Windows only.

http://www.retrofitproductions.com/level-director/

Lua Glider

Lua Glider is a coding environment you can use to write your Corona SDK programs. It comes with code completion and easy debugging tools, and it lets you set breakpoints during the execution of your programs. You can also send remote events to the simulator so that you can test the accelerometer without having to transfer your programs to your mobile device. It works on both Windows and Mac OS.

http://www.mydevelopersgames.com/CIDER/index.html

A1.3 Art Resources

Some programmers find creating art the most annoying part of game development. If that's the case for you, don't worry. You can make great games without having to draw a single sprite. Take a look at the following sites, where you can find a variety of free game art and particle-generation tools.

Ari Feldman's SpriteLib

Most game developers have used Ari Feldman's SpriteLib at some point. The library has a lot of graphics that you can use for your games, especially for top-down tank or airplane games. Even if you don't want to use these graphics for your commercial games, they're great for prototyping.

http://www.widgetworx.com/widgetworx/portfolio/spritelib.html

Reiner's Tilesets

This website is great for any tile-based development projects. Reiner's website has a lot of dimetric tiles (in the 4:3 ratio): buildings, character sprites, and environment props. You can use them to prototype your games.

http://www.reinerstilesets.de/

OpenGameArt

OpenGameArt is a fantastic source of free graphics for your games. You can find all types of 2D images: user-interface designs, icons, animated sprites, tile sets, and even fonts.

http://opengameart.org/

Lost Garden

If you need sprites to prototype your games, Daniel Cook's sets at Lost Garden are great. He has a lot of collections available under a Creative Commons Attribution 3.0 license. In this book, we've used some of his tiles, but he has spaceships, explosions, interface designs, and lots of other goodies.

http://www.lostgarden.com/

Particle Candy

Particle Candy is a particle-effects library that you can add to your Corona development projects. It generates particles during runtime so users won't get tired of seeing the same explosion animations again and again. Since it's Lua-based, you can use it on both Mac and Windows.

http://www.x-pressive.com/ParticleCandy_Corona/

TimelineFX Particle Effects Editor

We can't deny that adding particle effects to games makes them look more polished. Sometimes we can generate particles during runtime, and it's great, but what if our memory resources are limited and we have to use premade particles? The TimelineFX editor lets us create lots of particle animations and export them as sprite sheets so that we can use them in our games. It works on both Mac and Windows.

http://www.rigzsoft.co.uk/

Explosion Generator

You sometimes need cool explosion effects for your games, but it's important to keep explosion sprites varied. For this, an explosion generator can be a great tool, especially if it's free. Cliff Harris has several sprite sheets on his website, and he also distributes the explosion generator that he coded. Mac users can use the premade explosion sprites available on the website, and Windows users can generate their own using the explosion generator.

http://www.positech.co.uk/content/explosion/explosiongenerator.html

A1.4 Game Sounds

Playing a mute game isn't fun, so game sounds are very important in a distributable game. It's difficult to find good-quality free sounds that can be used in games; here you'll find a list of websites with reasonable prices so that development teams with tight budgets can use them too.

Soundsnap

Soundsnap has an amazing number of sound effects and short sounds. If there's anything you want to add to your game, then you'll probably find it here. On this site, you pay per download, not per sound purchased. That means you'll have to save your downloads because if you lose them, then you have to pay for them again.

http://www.soundsnap.com/

Soundrangers

Soundrangers comes with several sound effects and music loops that you can use for your games. It has thousands of sound effects, so you can find sounds for almost any type of game.

http://www.soundrangers.com/

AudioJungle

This website is part of the Envato Marketplace, and you can find many music styles in it. There are dozens of talented musicians, and you can listen to their work before buying anything. License terms are clear, and one music track costs a different amount depending on whether you want to create a commercial game or a free one. You can also find sound effects, but they are sometimes more expensive than those from other sites.

http://audiojungle.net/

Classes in Corona

We've used classes throughout this book, but Lua needs us to use our own class system if we want to use them. Here you can take a look at the inner workings of the class system we've used throughout the book.

To use this class system, do the following:

- Define a new class using MyClassName = Class(base). Change MyClassName to the class name you want to use, such as Ship or Hero. The base variable is optional and indicates the parent class you want to inherit from.

- Add a function to the class normally, using function myFunctionName(parameters) ... end.

- Create a new instance of the class using myInstance = MyClassName(parameters).

- Call a parent function of the class using ParentClassName.functionName(), such as Rocket.launch(self, parameters).

```
class.lua
-- Saves you from typing super() in each child class constructor
--    Set to false to call them manually
local waterfallConstructors = true

function Class( base )
    -- Initialize a new class instance
    local instanceFunctions = { }

    -- Save a reference to the base class (for inheritance purposes)
    if base then
        instanceFunctions.base = base
    end

    -- Super function (finds a parent function)
    findSuperFunction = function( self, value, ... )
```

```lua
        -- Loop until we find the closest "super" function
        --   or we run out of parent classes
        local base = self.instanceFunctions.base
        local tempBase = base
        while tempBase ~= nil do
            functionName = tempBase[value]
            if ( functionName ~= nil ) then
                return functionName
            end
            tempBase = tempBase.base
        end

        -- Return nil if there isn't a parent function
        return nil
end

-- Call super (finds the super function and calls it)
callSuperFunction = function( self, ... )
    local value = debug.getinfo(2, "n").name
    local superFunctionName = findSuperFunction( self, value )
    if ( superFunctionName ~= nil ) then
        return superFunctionName( self, ... )
    end

    -- Return nil if there is no parent function
    return nil
end

-- Index function. Seek function names, properties,
--   and parent class functions
seekVariable = function( self, value, ... )
    -- Check if we're looking for an existing function
    local functionName = self.instanceFunctions[value]
    local superFunctionName = findSuperFunction( self, value )

    -- Check if it's a function, a parent function, or a property
    if value == 'instanceFunctions' or value == 'base'
      or not functionName then
        -- Value is not a function for this class.
        --   Check if it's a function in the parent class
        if value == 'base' then
            -- Return the base
            return self.instanceFunctions.base
        elseif superFunctionName ~= nil then
            -- Return the parent class function
            return superFunctionName
        else
            -- Return the variable
            return rawget( self, value )
        end
```

```lua
    else
        -- It's a function. Return it
        return functionName
    end
end


-- Define a constructor to build an instance using ClassName( params )
local callMetamethod = { }

-- Constructor function. Calls constructor and parent constructors
callMetamethod.__call = function( self, ... )
    -- Make an instance and add the __index
    --  metamethod to call its functions
    local instance = { }
    instance.instanceFunctions = instanceFunctions
    indexmetamethod = { }
    indexmetamethod.__index = seekVariable
    setmetatable( instance, indexmetamethod )

    -- Super function
    instance.super = callSuperFunction

    -- Constructor queue (oldest first)
    local constructors = {}

    -- Add this constructor to the queue
    if instanceFunctions.new then
        constructors[ #constructors + 1 ] = instanceFunctions.new
    end

    if waterfallConstructors == true then
        --Add base/super constructors to the queue
        local tempBase = base
        local tempCurrent = instance
        while tempBase ~= nil do
            if tempBase.new and tempBase.new
                ~= tempCurrent.new then
                    -- Call the base constructor if it exists
                    constructors[ #constructors + 1 ] =
                        tempBase.new
                    tempCurrent = tempBase
            end
            tempBase = tempBase.base
        end
    end

    -- Call the constructors. Oldest first.
    for i = #constructors, 1, -1 do
        constructors[i]( instance, ... )
    end
```

```lua
        -- Return the instance
        return instance
    end

    -- Set the meta table for the instance function
    --   so that a new class can be made using ClassName( )
    setmetatable( instanceFunctions, callMetamethod )
    return instanceFunctions
end
```

Index

3D for Kids and iOS Testing

Kids! Write 3D games in JavaScript. Grown-ups! Learn all about testing user interfaces on iOS devices.

You know what's even better than playing games? Creating your own. Even if you're an absolute beginner, this book will teach you how to make your own online games with interactive examples. You'll learn programming using nothing more than a browser, and see cool, 3D results as you type. You'll learn real-world programming skills in a real programming language: Java-Script, the language of the web. You'll be amazed at what you can do as you build interactive worlds and fun games.

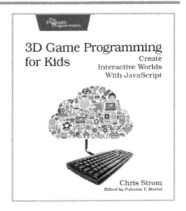

Chris Strom
(250 pages) ISBN: 9781937785444. $36
http://pragprog.com/book/csjava

If you're an iOS developer or QA professional tapping through an app to reproduce bugs or performance issues you thought were solved two releases ago, then this is your book. Learn how to script the user interface, assert correct behavior, stub external dependencies, reproduce performance problems, organize test code for the long haul, and automate the whole process so the machine does the work. You'll walk through a comprehensive strategy with techniques using Apple's tools that you can apply to your own apps.

Jonathan Penn
(226 pages) ISBN: 9781937785529. $36
http://pragprog.com/book/jptios

Sound and Graphics

Add live sound to your mobile and web apps, and deep dive into OpenGL on Android devices.

Sound gives your native, web, or mobile apps that extra dimension, and it's essential for games. Rather than using canned samples from a sample library, learn how to build sounds from the ground up and produce them for web projects using the Pure Data programming language. Even better, you'll be able to integrate dynamic sound environments into your native apps or games—sound that reacts to the app, instead of sounding the same every time. Start your journey as a sound designer, and get the power to craft the sound you put into your digital experiences.

Tony Hillerson
(200 pages) ISBN: 9781937785666. $36
http://pragprog.com/book/thsound

Android is booming like never before, with millions of devices shipping every day. It's never been a better time to learn how to create your own 3D games and live wallpaper for Android. You'll find out all about shaders and the OpenGL pipeline, and discover the power of OpenGL ES 2.0, which is much more feature-rich than its predecessor. If you can program in Java and you have a creative vision that you'd like to share with the world, then this is the book for you.

Kevin Brothaler
(346 pages) ISBN: 9781937785345. $38
http://pragprog.com/book/kbogla

The Pragmatic Bookshelf

The Pragmatic Bookshelf features books written by developers for developers. The titles continue the well-known Pragmatic Programmer style and continue to garner awards and rave reviews. As development gets more and more difficult, the Pragmatic Programmers will be there with more titles and products to help you stay on top of your game.

Visit Us Online

This Book's Home Page
http://pragprog.com/book/sdcorona
Source code from this book, errata, and other resources. Come give us feedback, too!

Register for Updates
http://pragprog.com/updates
Be notified when updates and new books become available.

Join the Community
http://pragprog.com/community
Read our weblogs, join our online discussions, participate in our mailing list, interact with our wiki, and benefit from the experience of other Pragmatic Programmers.

New and Noteworthy
http://pragprog.com/news
Check out the latest pragmatic developments, new titles and other offerings.

Save on the eBook

Save on the eBook versions of this title. Owning the paper version of this book entitles you to purchase the electronic versions at a terrific discount.

PDFs are great for carrying around on your laptop—they are hyperlinked, have color, and are fully searchable. Most titles are also available for the iPhone and iPod touch, Amazon Kindle, and other popular e-book readers.

Buy now at *http://pragprog.com/coupon*

Contact Us

Online Orders:	*http://pragprog.com/catalog*
Customer Service:	*support@pragprog.com*
International Rights:	*translations@pragprog.com*
Academic Use:	*academic@pragprog.com*
Write for Us:	*http://pragprog.com/write-for-us*
Or Call:	+1 800-699-7764

CPSIA information can be obtained at www.ICGtesting.com
Printed in the USA
LVOW02s1037111113

360811LV00004B/6/P